Mommyblogs and the Changing Face of Motherhood

Mothers have consistently relied upon one another for guidance and support as they navigate the difficult world of parenting. For many women, the increasingly established online community of "mommyblogs" now provides a source of camaraderie and support that acknowledges both the work of mothering and the implications of its undertaking. But beyond their capacity to entertain, how have mommyblogs shifted our understanding of twenty-first-century motherhood?

In examining the content of hundreds of mommyblogs, May Friedman considers the ways that online maternal life writing provides a front row seat to some of the most raw, offbeat, and engaging portraits of motherhood imaginable. Focusing on the composition of the "mamasphere" and on mommyblogs' emphasis on connection, Friedman reveals the changing face of contemporary motherhood – one less concerned with the proscriptions of what good mothers should do, and more invested in what diverse mothers have to say.

MAY FRIEDMAN is an assistant professor in the School of Social Work at Ryerson University.

MAY FRIEDMAN

Mommyblogs and the Changing Face of Motherhood

UNIVERSITY OF TORONTO PRESS
Toronto Buffalo London

© University of Toronto Press 2013
Toronto Buffalo London
www.utppublishing.com
Printed in Canada

ISBN 978-1-4426-4624-7 (cloth)
ISBN 978-1-4426-1430-7 (paper)

∞

Printed on acid-free, 100% post-consumer recycled paper with vegetable-based inks.

Library and Archives Canada Cataloguing in Publication

Friedman, May, 1975–
Mommyblogs and the changing face of motherhood / May Friedman.

Includes bibliographical references and index.
ISBN 978-1-4426-4624-7 (bound). – ISBN 978-1-4426-1430-7 (pbk.)

1. Mothers – Blogs.   2. Motherhood – Blogs.   3. Parenting – Blogs.
4. Blogs – Social aspects.   I. Title.

HQ759.F75 2013   306.874'3028567   C2012-905900-5

This book has been published with the help of a grant from the
Canadian Federation for the Humanities and Social Sciences, through
the Awards to Scholarly Publications Program, using funds provided
by the Social Sciences and Humanities Research Council of Canada.

University of Toronto Press acknowledges the financial assistance to its
publishing program of the Canada Council for the Arts and the Ontario
Arts Council.

University of Toronto Press acknowledges the financial support of the
Government of Canada through the Canada Book Fund for its publishing activities.

To Dan, for always being a safe place to land

Contents

Acknowledgments

It takes a village to write a book, and I've had the great good fortune of having several villages' worth of support throughout this process.

In the academic realm, without the work of the Motherhood Initiative for Research and Community Involvement (MIRCI, formerly the Association for Research on Mothering), I would have floundered in the isolation of new motherhood far longer, rather than seeing my suspicions about motherhood reflected, amplified, and constantly, deliciously, discussed. MIRCI's "mama," Dr Andrea O'Reilly, not only provided, in MIRCI, a superlative incubator for my academic growth, but also acted as an exceptional supervisor, mentor, and friend, and to her I give my huge thanks. My new academic home in the School of Social Work at Ryerson University likewise deserves thanks for support and camaraderie, as does Ryerson's Faculty of Community Services for their generous provision of a publication grant. I am also so appreciative of Beth McAuley, who provided editing genius and moral support and truly gave this project the makeover it required.

The Feminist Mothers Group has held me close and constantly pushed my thinking further and I am indebted to them for every word. To my dear friends, especially Emma Lind, Anna Korteweg and Jim Davis, and Marcia Beck, I give my great thanks for cheerleading, pizza, and thoughtful interjections at just the right moments. I give enormous thanks also for the loving support of my families, Uzi and Shula Dalume, Rose and Rubin Friedman, and all the sibs and cousins.

Finally, to my muses: thanks to Noah, Molly, and Isaac, for keeping me frantic and calming me down, over and over again; and to Dan, for holding my hand, reading my words, and being my partner in all things.

Mommyblogs and the Changing Face of Motherhood

1 Introduction

I just want to be old one day, in a rocker with a cool glass of lemonade (or perhaps gin), flipping through my mental Rolodex of perfect moments . . .
— Catherine Newman, *Bringing Up Ben and Birdy*[1]

Thus began the first blog I ever read, on my travels towards motherhood. In my pregnant and slowly expanding state, the words of a woman I didn't know seemed to hold the key to the secret reality that awaited me. I couldn't imagine the shift in identity that lay before me, and as an apprehensive traveller to this uncharted territory, I looked to blogs – part welcome mat, part travel guide – to ease my trepidation. But I did not yet understand how central blogs written by mothers would be to my development, as both a person and a parent. I read these texts alongside more traditional pregnancy and parenting books, while dutifully attending prenatal classes.

Finally becoming a mother nine years ago transformed me almost as greatly as my own birth. I was shocked by the demands put on me, the depth of my love for this new being, the ways all of my close relationships were transformed, and the extent to which my selfhood was called into question. Some of these transformations were due to the ceaseless work of new parenting; as I took on the majority of the care for a helpless creature, my relationship to concepts like "leisure" and "privacy" shifted dramatically. Yet the biggest shift in my sense of self came from my entrance into the hallowed realm of Motherhood, from the insistence by those around me that now I *must* be different and that my prior self was simply irrelevant. In those early days I lacked the language to express my bewilderment at the stripping down of subjectivity that I was witnessing – by the baby, as I might have expected, but also by my friends, my own mother, and the world at large. Motherhood thus led me to an identity crisis that I had not anticipated. As a feminist academic I sought out feminist writing on motherhood so I could begin to understand the seismic shift that was occurring, and read work by Adrienne Rich (1976), Sara Ruddick (1980), and Naomi Wolf (2001). While much feminist writing had resonance (for example, Thurer, 1994; Hays, 1998; Maushart, 2000),

I found it did not yield the intimacy and dialogue that I craved. Even the best academic writing had a conclusion, which – in keeping with all expert literature on motherhood – was often presented as a "right" way to mother. Now, in addition to being bewildered, I was also frustrated that I could not maintain my feminist idealism when it came down to the messy, real-life work of parenting.

Isolated and house-bound with my infant, I craved companionship. I turned on my computer, looking for a representation of my experience, for writing that somehow resonated with my frustrations and ambivalence. I returned to the writing that had kept me company throughout my pregnancy, encouraged to find the dialogue increasing exponentially as each author linked to more. I leapt hungrily from blog to blog, following links and references, thrilled to confirm that I was not the only new mother feeling as I did. In turning to the mamasphere for wisdom, I found women who were keepers of real-life experiences that soothed me, calmed my fears, and presented their own contradictions and ambiguities.

The blogs I first encountered were not written by women who self-identified as feminists. Rather, many of the women bloggers I initially encountered were fun and fearless. Take, for example, the iconic women behind *Dooce* and *Mimi Smartypants*, popular blogs known across many cyber-realms. As these women became mothers, they turned their trademark irreverence to this new identity and terrain. Even my old favourite blog, *Bringing Up Ben and Birdy* by feminist and former academic Catherine Newman, was of value more for its wry hilarity than its explicit political strides. Mimi Smartypants noted some of the bizarre behavioural shifts that motherhood wreaks:

> One of the strangest things about motherhood is the constant stream of words that flows out of you. Were there not a small child near me, people would be shaking their heads sadly at my schizophrenic monologues about putting on "our" shoes, why eating the cat is not a good idea, and how we knocked down the blocks, yes we did! Wow! That was great! . . . since I am new at this mommy thing I am still kind of self-conscious about the running commentary on everything we saw along the way ("Look Nora! An empty condom box! And a dead bird! Well, most of a dead bird.")[2]

More succinctly, Heather Armstrong of *Dooce* chronicles saying goodbye before leaving her child with her mother overnight: "Leta took one look at all the toys in Grandma's basement and forgot that she ever shot out my crotch."[3] On a darker note, like many other readers, I watched the unspiralling of Heather's postpartum depression in real time. I felt a kinship to this mother that I lacked in the embodied world of parents around me.

In these and the many other blogs I discovered online, I found a convoluted wisdom born of myriad accounts of motherhood. Each individual blogger told her story and while there was much that I dis-agreed with – for example, normative gender roles, subtle racism and homophobia, certain specifics of parenting practice – I nonetheless found that the depth of narrative and intimacy in each account gave me insights into different parenting choices and practices. In addition to these "thick" accounts of life and mothering,[4] I was intrigued by the many non-normative mothers and parenting practices that I was find-ing online, as well as the burgeoning community I was witnessing as many bloggers began to create a shared and dialogic account of moth-ering. As a long-time reader of life writing, this new format fed my insatiable curiosity about how mothers lived, extending that hunger to first-person accounts by providing an increasingly relational nar-rative. The intimacy, diversity, and community of the mamasphere quickly made me an avid reader and, while the selection of blogs I fol-low has shifted considerably over time, I consider reading these blogs to be an important part of my self-development as an individual and as a parent. Over the years, I have shared many blogs with my part-ner and others and, as a result, have opened many conversations that led to a more self-reflexive parenting style. Blogs have also helped me confront my own contradictions and overlaid identities, as I was re-minded in a blog post by Catherine Newman, now blogging at *Dalai Mama Dishes*:

There is not much that makes me feel more happily maternal than baking a small cake on a weeknight.

And now I'm starting a new paragraph, because that sentence really needs to be left all alone up there. Maybe some of my hundreds of UC Santa Cruz feminist theory students circa 1992–1999 will come upon this, and they'll remember my motorcycle boots and my hockey skates and my badass politics, and they'll be all *What the*? They'll be all, *Hello Professor Mrs. Brady*. But I swear, I'm still that exact same person (minus boots and skates). It's just that there's something so delightful about welcoming my family to the table when there's a *cake on a plate*. The children always oooh and aaah like orphans peeping in a bakery window, and I could kiss those rosy urchin cheeks. And do.[5]

As a feminist mother who regularly uses Newman's plum cake recipe; as a brown mother of white children; and as an educated, class-privileged woman from a working-class background, I find myself drawn to the contradictions of the blogosphere, to its intimacy and multivariousness. For me, finding and reading these blogs has been a way to celebrate the ceaselessly complicated maternal subject; a way to interrupt the story of motherhood – whether patriarchal, empowered, feminist, or otherwise – and present it as far from simple. Mommyblogs gave me a response to the story of motherhood told from the outside and instead showed me motherhood, and mothers, from within.

The Emergence of Networked Communication and the Birth of Blogs

Without going into an exhaustive history, I briefly consider here the swift rise of the World Wide Web that led to the explosion of blogs as a medium for online life writing; in chapter 2, I look more extensively at the role of life writing and the genesis of blogging practice.

The infancy of the Internet saw the creation of more and more networked possibilities for communication in the form of nascent electronic mail and messaging capabilities, as well as through broader forms of communication between groups of people. Beginning in 1989 with the advent of the first dial-up Internet Service Provider (at that time serving only the eastern United States), technically proficient computer users began to consider the possible uses of networked computers on a much greater scale. By 1991 the World Wide Web had taken hold, and along with it came an increasing number of nontechnical users who were building "sites" online. One of these early online protocols was Bulletin Board Systems (some of which dated back to the 1970s), which allowed users to interact with distant computers and, as a result, the users of those computers. The major users of BBS were professional or amateur computer programmers who discussed technical solutions to computer problems. These bulletin boards quickly morphed into special interest boards that featured multidirectional communication around a range of topics, including "politics, religion, music, dating, and alternative lifestyles."[6] Increasingly, bulletin boards came to resemble more traditional communities, with the same supports and tensions that "real life" (RL) communities tended to show. Internet users had the BBS with which to form connections, but they craved a more personal web presence, which led to the creation of personal home pages. These sites not only showcased the interests and personalities of their authors (or "netizens"), but also provided links to others sites on the web. Even though these links were not organized in any way, personal home pages began to hint at the capacity for interconnectivity, and by the early to mid-1990s, a few netizens began to conceive of their homepages predominantly as places to list links to other sites they found interesting or important, while sometimes including ongoing commentary.

The line between writing commentary about links and writing personal analysis or introspection was not crossed in a clear moment, but Carolyn Burke's 1995 decision to write an online account of the end of an intimate relationship opened the door to a different type of online writing (Podnicks, 2002, p. 125). Burke had created an online diary, which shifted the focus of traditional diary writing into a public form of life writing and opened up the possibility of interaction and commentary. Laurie McNeill (2003) argues that "while the term 'online diaries' clearly connects these texts to the print world, to the traditions of the diary and the generic rules and expectations that come with them, the expression 'blogs' invites a reading of these writings as a 'new artform' (Schalchlin), one without the cultural baggage of an existing (print) genre" (p. 29). McNeill's analysis of the shift in genre, however, describes an organic shift from one term to another and notes that for many writers, the two formats bled seamlessly into one another.

At the same time, certain traits within these online journals were privileged: there was an "increasingly common reverse chronological organization and the central role of links, but also a focus outward toward information on the wider Web, rather than inward on personal experience" (Rosenberg, 2009, p. 87). As well, these journals began to be organized into "webrings" that would bring together readers and writers who chose to connect on given topics or through the use of a given technology (for example, webrings for large families, or a Perl programming language webring). These webrings began to create the community and dialogism that characterize blogs and social networking sites on today's Internet, but it took some time before they shared a common name. For a while, some were considered weblogs but others used the titles "linklists," "newspages," or "filters" (Rosenberg, 2009, p. 87).

In 1999, only four years after Carolyn Burke wrote the first online journal entry, two occurrences solidified the word "blog" as the preferred title for privately authored sites (as opposed to corporate sites) that collected both links and personal musings. In May of 1999, Peter Merholz shifted the word weblog and noted, "I've decided to pronounce the word 'weblog' as 'wee-blog.' Or 'blog' for short" (quoted in Rosenberg, 2009, p. 102). Merholz's usage was quirky and catered to the in-joke sensibility that characterized the early Internet. Furthermore, his shift from "weblog" to "we blog" – something that "we" did – allowed for the progression of the word from noun to verb, a pleasing syntactic contortion that further led to the word's popularity.

Nonetheless, *"blog* would probably have languished as an obscure neologism" had it not been for a tiny Internet startup called Pyra: "In August 1999, they unveiled a little side project called Blogger. The fruit of a week's worth of programming labor, Blogger was a free tool for automating the updating of personal weblogs. It took off almost immediately, and its success made the blog label stick" (Rosenberg, 2009, p. 102). The Blogger application itself was an instant success. By early 2000, the company had 2,300 accounts; by 2002, there were over 700,000 (Rosenberg, 2009, pp. 115, 125). While there was a proliferation of software for early webloggers to choose from, Blogger coined the term that stuck for this new medium; it also saw a level of success (if not prosperity) unrivalled by other early self-publishing programs such as Pitas and Diaryland (Blood, 2000; Rosenberg, 2009). Perhaps more importantly, by automating a process that had heretofore required hand-coding (albeit in a limited and relatively user-friendly fashion), Blogger pushed online self-publishing beyond the realm of computer programmers and hackers. While certain characteristics of the early blogs remained (reverse chronology chief among them), widened access to blogging technology and the sheer proliferation of users that resulted led the scope of topics to explode.

Even in the infancy of networked life writing, such writing was viewed as theoretically important. Linda Warley (2005, p. 32), in her discussion of online journals, noted that such writing was distinct from its analogue counterpart largely due to its interactivity and multimodality; that is, its capacity for instant connection and its reliance on text coupled with pictures, textures, and colours in order to achieve a more multisensory experience. Podnieks (2004) goes further in discussing the capacity for relationality in these early blogs, arguing, "In online diaries, each mouse-click and each entry generates the text, the graphics and even the sound that says 'I communicate, therefore I am'" (p. 144). Podnieks cautions against unnecessarily valorizing blogs and their forebears as radically new, noting that handwritten and print diaries and journals were often circulated among friends and family and existed much more in the public sphere than is often considered. Furthermore, print diaries would, in some instances, allow for the same capacity as their online counterparts in illuminating generally unremarkable and unexamined lives. Rosenwald (1988) notes that "diaries have followed autobiographies in becoming not so much books published as intimate guides to famous men and women as books published by men and women interested in becoming famous" (p. 11). While fame may be the motive for some mothers who write blogs, McNeill (2003) suggests an alternative motivation: "The online diary, in which the writing and the written subject seem to occupy the same moment as each other and as the reader, already creates a sense of congruency between the lived and the written" (p. 40). This practice of networked life writing on-line has created a collective of mothers who write shared experiences about mothering and, in the process, have built a sense of community and congruency. This cyberworld has come to be known as the mama-sphere, and this genre of blogs are now known as mommyblogs.

An examination of the Internet presents virtually infinite possible questions. Looking at the blogosphere and focusing on the mama-sphere results in a narrowed focus but still allows for an extremely broad range of questions, considerations, and points of entry. Mommy-blogs are exemplified by their differences – they chronicle different ex-periences, use different forms of blogging software, and often include aspects of life outside the realm of motherhood. They are created and extinguished continuously, such that any preliminary criteria that cir-cumscribe today's mommyblogs may be negated by those of tomor-row. Nonetheless, this disparate and ragged grouping has cohered into a vibrant, dynamic, and multifarious collective.

Mommyblogs: The Term

Any analysis of mommyblogs as a cultural phenomenon must begin, by necessity, with a deconstruction of the terminology. How did moth-ering practice come to be subsumed under the patronizing mantle of "mommyhood"? Susan Douglas and Meredith Michaels (2004) bemoan the rise of "the new momism," arguing that "'Mom' – a term previously used only by children – doesn't have the authority of 'mother,' because it addresses us from a child's-eye view . . . " (p. 19). Douglas and Mi-chaels's critique has great resonance in the realm of the blogosphere, where few areas of women's life writing have emerged as powerfully as have accounts of parenting and family life. Of more concern is that often women's life writing that mentions mothering in any respect is immediately reduced to "mommy" writing, reminding us, as Douglas and Michaels (2004) argue, that "'Mom' sounds very user-friendly, but the rise of it, too, keeps us in our place, reminding us that we are defined by our relationships to kids, not to adults" (pp. 19–20). Furthermore, as many bloggers note, the terminology is also deeply gendered, ensuring that women are defined by family life in ways that are simply not applied to fathers.

Despite these concerns, in the face of the wholesale definition of this group of blogs by the term "mommyblog," to avoid it would be ineffective. As Shana Calixte and I wrote in the introduction to *Mothering and Blogging: The Radical Act of the Mommyblog,*

> The extent to which the term [mommyblogger] has organically emerged as the *de facto* terminology of reference cannot be underestimated. A quick Google search for "mother bloggers" yields fewer than two thousand hits, while a search for "mommybloggers" brings up over eighty thousand hits. To refer to this genre by any other name, then, is potentially disingenuous, and, in an era so overwhelmingly powered by the search engine, may result in the burying of blogs who seek to rescue this medium from the taint of patriarchal motherhood. (Friedman & Calixte, 2009, p. 25)

Many mommybloggers have embraced the term precisely as an ironic reclamation, an attempt to resist the supposition that everything they have to say is about motherhood. Indeed, the frustrations about monetization and authenticity that have emerged as points of controversy among blogging mothers (touched upon in the conclusion of this book) reveal the extent to which many mommybloggers value the rich intimacy of blogging practice. Yet in embracing this term a further ambiguity is highlighted, as "mommies" are presenting themselves in a dynamic context that ensures they are not easily reduced to their parenting tasks. Is there room for mommybloggers to equally reclaim the term "mommy" and convey the richness of maternal lives? Or is this dynamism evident only from within the mamasphere, invisible to outsiders who maintain that such blogs are steadfastly limited to stories about children and poop?

There exists at least the potential for a notable shift wherein the depth of archive of each maternal life actively resists the positioning of motherhood as an exclusive identity category, subsuming all other aspects of subjectivity. Though mommyblogger, as an identity category, is unlikely to create a seismic shift in understandings of mothers, the term can be seen as potentially robust and interesting, and may provide templates for the directions in which "mother" might move over time.

Why Do Mothers Blog?

Mommyblogging stands in stark contrast to that other suburban maternal pursuit: scrapbooking. Whether physical or digital, scrapbooks focus on children, documenting and producing an artefact of their early lives. By contrast, mommyblogs capture *maternal* experiences, give mothers a voice, and foster conversation and participation in a community, the beginnings of a response to Sara Ruddick's (1989) assertion that mothers are so often left out of the story (p. 11). This practice thus provides a necessary antidote to maternal isolation, but it also provides validation that maternal experiences – and not simply documentations of childhood – are valid and worthy of discussion. Like consciousness-raising groups of the past, mothers who blog have room to dissect their own experience in chorus, to (potentially, at least) find the political in the shared personal and examine their lives critically. Paul John Eakin (1999) draws on the work of psychologist John Shotter in suggesting that such writing exists at the moment wherein "the 'I' . . . is 'interpellated' by the 'you'" (p. 63).

The mamasphere challenges the stability of the mother subject. In using life writing as "a critical practice" (Kadar, 1992), mommybloggers are able to construct a more nuanced and contradictory maternal subject. There are five key characteristics that allow them this capacity. Their blogs are

- diverse in terms of social location and maternal experience,
- multitudinous in their participation by vast numbers of mothers,[7]
- relational in their focus on dialogue and interactivity across blogs,
- atemporal by allowing for a linking back into the past and the evolution of an unending narrative, and
- performative in sharing mothers' lived experiences in opposition to prescriptive expert discourses.

It is these attributes of the mamasphere (all of which draw on and extend the rich history of life writing and motherhood writing) that allow mothers writing online to participate in a new form of maternal subjectivity. They are creating a form of maternal thought that is rich and interpersonal while at the same time full of contradictions and confusions, providing an analysis of maternal experiences that is not found in more traditional, linear, and stable narratives.

By acknowledging the chaos of women's lived experiences as mothers through their own words, mommybloggers are mastering a method that has strong roots in motherhood studies. They are reaching out through their life writings to "create a collective description of the world" (Rich, 1976) that can support and nourish as well as criticize and challenge what they do. As Adrienne Rich wrote in *Of Woman Born*,

> For many months I buried my head in historical research and analysis in order to delay or prepare the way for the plunge into areas of my own life that were painful and problematical, yet from the heart of which this book has come. I believe increasingly that only the willingness to share private and sometimes painful experience can enable women to create a collective description of the world which will be truly ours. (1976, pp. 15–16)

In her essay "In Search of Our Mothers' Gardens," Alice Walker (1974) takes these connections further, suggesting that there is much to gain by considering our mothers' stories as the sources of our wisdom and continuity. She writes,

> So many of the stories that I write, that we all write, are my mother's stories. Only recently did I fully realize this: that through years of listening to my mother's stories of her life, I have absorbed not only the stories themselves, but something of the manner in which she spoke, something of the urgency that involves the knowledge that her stories – like her life – must be recorded. (p. 93)

In looking at the "private and painful experience" of motherhood, at various mothers' stories over time, mommyblogs provide an amazing portrait of the compelling, convoluted, and contradictory terrain of mothers and motherhood in the early twenty-first century, a portrait undertaken by vast realms of women that can be shared simultaneously. The presence of a collectively authored and endlessly evolving account of maternal life presents relationality squared: Mothers create shared accounts by engaging in dialogue about mothering, and are also presenting, in those accounts, evidence of the entwined nature of maternal work, the endless connections between mothers and children.

Such an account presents a very real threat to the myth of the individual human subject.

In describing this relational politic, it is important to skirt precisely the trap that mothers are often pushed towards: the concretization of motherhood as a natural and static condition with a concomitant natural morality and knowledge, which can somehow be plundered in order to heal the troubled world. Rather, by looking at mothers, who are often required to perform relational labour, we may consider the ways that, from infancy, all humans function as relational individuals, and also consider the relationships that exist beyond the dyad of mother and child. By beginning to view motherhood as simply one example of the relationality we all experience, we may shift towards a postmodern view that sees our liminal subjects as continuously overlapping rather than discretely and fixedly sitting side by side.

Mielle Chandler (2007) takes up the idea of maternal subjectivity in the context of a politics of individualism, arguing that the focus on women's autonomous empowerment that characterizes much feminist theory foregrounds individuality and is thus inconsistent with the lived experience of motherhood. She suggests, instead, that society acknowledge mothers as subjects "in-relation" and that "the problematic lies not in the equation of motherhood with non-subjectivity but in the privileging of an emancipated individuated subjectivity" (p. 535). Chandler's insights provide possibilities for a relational understanding of the maternal subject that acknowledges both the intrinsically dyadic nature of parenting vulnerable children who are unable to care for themselves and the implications of mothering undertaken in community and described in dialogue.

Such an insight makes sense not only of individual experiences of parenting but also of the emergent community exposed in the mamasphere. Drawing from Andrea O'Reilly's (2008a) insights about the four "a's" of empowered mothering (agency, authority, autonomy, and authenticity) (p. 11), the hybridity of the mamasphere (discussed in chapter 3) allows for a complicated empowerment, one that draws on two further "a's": ambiguity and ambivalence. This confusion is born of both the wealth of maternal accounts that exist online as well as the depth of each individual story, leading to a fractured and incoherent subjectivity. The mamasphere thus presents a view of the maternal subject that draws on feminist motherhood studies but extends this understanding even further in its focus on the maternal subject as relational and ambiguous.

What Mommyblogs Offer

If, in Rich's terms, mothers are caught between the patriarchal institution of motherhood and the mothering practice that they undertake, mommyblogs provide infinite examples of the incredible shackles of the dominant discourses of motherhood presented as a selfless natural state, interrupted continuously by account after account of mothering shown as hard, raw work.

Rich (1976) presented this distinction between institution and practice of motherhood initially in *Of Woman Born*, writing of

> the *potential relationship* of any woman to her powers of reproduction and to children; and the *institution*, which aims at ensuring that that potential – and all women – shall remain under male control. This institution has been a keystone of the most diverse social and political systems. It has withheld over one half of the human species from the decisions affecting their lives; it exonerates men from fatherhood in any authentic sense; it creates the dangerous schism between "private" and "public" life; it calcifies human choices and potentialities. In the most fundamental and bewildering of contradictions, it has alienated women from our bodies by incarcerating us in them. (p. 13)

Rich's distinction remains intensely relevant. Mothering is still taking place within the context of patriarchal motherhood, and the distinction – between the specific work that mothers *do* and who mothers *are*, as well as the specific constraints placed on women's lives as mothers – is all too often ignored. To ignore this distinction is to expect women to grin and bear all that is unbearable about motherhood. Rich's insights were groundbreaking, allowing as they did the distinction between the work done by mothers and the dominant discourse of patriarchy guiding this work. Her ideas have since been taken up and developed by many motherhood scholars. By suggesting that women's dissatisfaction with motherhood might be due to the imposition of misogynist expectations and demands, and not the biology of mothering itself, Rich allowed for the possibility of a reclamation of motherhood, a way for mothering to be undertaken in an enjoyable and empowering way. Interestingly, Rich arrives at this conclusion through the lens of her own experience. Writing in a style reminiscent of many mommybloggers, Rich writes of a vacation from her husband and, as a result, from the constraints of expectations of "appropriate" motherhood:

Driving home once, after midnight, from a late drive-in movie . . . with three sleeping children in the back of the car, I felt wide awake, elated; we had broken together all the rules of bedtime, the night rules, rules I myself thought I had to observe in the city or become a "bad mother." We were conspirators, outlaws from the institution of motherhood; I felt enormously in charge of my life. (1976, pp. 194–5)

In chronicling her escape, Rich clearly shows the cage in which she is trapped. By exposing the institution of motherhood, then, Rich is finally able to find possibilities beyond it. This distinction has greatly informed the wealth of motherhood literature that has burgeoned in the thirty-five years since Rich first put it forth. Rich's insights, and those of the powerful motherhood theorists who have followed, have created a groundwork for understanding maternity as a complicated subjectivity and a field of study ripe for analysis.

Mommyblogs present a lived tension between mothering and motherhood, between "good" and "bad" mothering, which allows for collisions to occur between these slippery and contested terrains. In their vast and unedited realms, mommyblogs reveal a self-reflexivity and an honest grappling that resists an easy label of "feminist" or "patriarchal." It is precisely this lived tension that mothers embody. While the theoretical possibilities of Rich's distinction have led motherhood studies to some critical and important realms, the time has come for an approach to motherhood that gives a closer examination of discourse and subjectivity, an analysis that stands on the shoulders of critical mothering theorists but extends their analysis even further. Such an analysis may defy easy conclusions, but it is not at all unproductive; rather, in looking at the lived tension between contradictory and confusing discourses of motherhood and the ways they are enacted, the complicated nature of maternal subjectivity and the significant complexities of the constraints and opportunities afforded mothers may be appreciated. Thirty-five years ago Rich's incisive distinction was required to push analyses of motherhood forward. In order to successfully examine motherhood in the twenty-first century, it is necessary to draw upon feminist insights about motherhood and extend the analysis even further, to consider the hybridity and confusion of the maternal subject.

In trying to form conclusions about mommybloggers – and about mothers – I am reminded of my children attempting to jump upon their own shadows: I am attempting to trap an essentially untrappable form of knowledge. After the initial discomfort and frustration that this inconclusive conclusion elicits, however, I have found that there is much to be gained, as a researcher in general and as a motherhood researcher in particular, in looking instead at uncertainty as a valuable critical lens. By showing the limitations of a framework that draws, in both theory and policy, from liberal modernism in its respect for individual human rights, the theoretical manifestations of hybrid, cyborg, and queer theory expressed in these online writings move us towards a relational politics that is both flexible and responsive to the convoluted and interactive lives that people are truly living.

Limitations of the Genre: The Digital Divide

The term "digital divide,"[8] defined as "the troubling gap between those who use computers and the Internet and those who do not" (Mehra, Merkel, & Bishop, 2004, p. 782), initially referred only to computer ownership; as Internet use has become more firmly embedded in the details of Western life, however, it has become a core component of the digital divide. Mehra, Merkel, and Bishop argue that race, class, and education are the key components that disallow some people from digital citizenry. These characteristics generally refer to a digital divide within industrialized nations, looking, for example, at the greater access to computers and the web among wealthy students in comparison to their poorer counterparts. Beyond this definition, however, there is an increasing discussion of the global digital divide – the lack of computer hardware and digital infrastructure that leaves much of the developing world unconnected. While there are emergent initiatives such as One Laptop per Child that aim to respond to the global digital divide, these are usually reliant on open-source software and operating systems that may, even at their best, still result in a two tier system of computer use, again entrenching the poverty and digital limitations of those in the Global South. Indeed, even in the developed world, the spread of wireless and high-speed Internet access has been slow and uneven, skewing access towards urban centres and arguably thus rendering the experiences of rural households less prominent.

The implications of the digital divide cannot be understated as computer access creates faster and thicker connections between privileged users and thus emphasizes and solidifies the poverty of non-Internet users at both a national and international level. Arguably, the digital divide is a key method for ensuring that the rich get richer while the poor fall deeper into poverty. Furthermore, beyond creating or facilitating jobs or affluence, the Internet is arguably the most powerful tool on the planet for creating knowledge. This knowledge is collectively produced and thus unstable; this is one of the Internet's great strengths. Yet the digital divide ensures that only some people's stories are told; knowledge production, while constantly debated, is skewed extraordinarily towards issues of concern to people experiencing privilege on the basis of social location while ignoring the lives and concerns of others. This is readily apparent in the mamasphere, which cannot begin to be seen as representative of the world's mothers. While the mamasphere provides a broad and diverse picture of an extremely wide range of mothers, an extraordinary number of mothering experiences are not documented there due to the digital divide. This would arguably be inevitable unless every mother in the world blogged, but it is important to recognize that the gaps in maternal experience online are not random; the mamasphere does not, for example, include the stories of every tenth person. Certain experiences are grossly overrepresented as a result of class and other privileges, while others – arguably those of the majority of mothers worldwide – are completely inaccessible to blog readers due to both technical and financial limitations at the individual and national levels. Furthermore, at least within the mamasphere, bloggers skew heavily towards youth; users over the age of forty are underrepresented.

While it is necessary to remain cognizant of the digital divide and its harrowing implications, it is also important to consider the extent to which the digital world has only intensified, rather than invented, tensions between classes, races, and nationalities. As Lisa Servon (2002) has written, the digital divide "is a symptom of a larger and more complex problem – the problem of persistent poverty and inequality" (p. 2); Rich reminds us "this is the oppressor's language yet I need it to talk to you" (quoted in Jackaman, 2003, p. 91). In addition, there are moments of hope, spaces where people who have been historically silenced or disenfranchised have found voice online. Lisa Ferris (2009), for example, writes,

I found writing online liberating for a number of reasons. It was a forum where I, a deafblind woman, could communicate on an equal footing. Communicating with people in real life is a constant struggle in which who I am – my thoughts, my intelligence, my grace and consideration, the essence of me – is lost in a physically exhausting struggle to simply keep track of what is going on around me. I sometimes feel like my personality is crushed by the failure of my vision and hearing to allow me to communicate in ways that people are familiar with. People who don't know me well seem to find me somewhere in a range between, at worst, mentally incompetent, or at best, quirky and discomforting. Online, by contrast, I found a small audience of intelligent peers who respected my opinions and engaged me in thoughtful discussions without regard to my disability. It was my nerdy secret social oasis. (p. 68)

Ferris notes the ways that the Internet has given her a voice and a community; for other users with the class privilege of Internet access but with non-normative social locations in other respects, online computer use has allowed community to transcend physical proximity and to maintain anonymity – this has led to virtually infinite possibilities for community and affinity groups online. While this does not negate the implications of the digital divide, nor does it excuse us from tirelessly working to minimize this problem, it is important to see the ways that Internet access has not precisely mimicked existing relations of power, dominance, and silence.

Authenticity: Do Mommyblogs Tell the Truth?

Arguing that mommyblogs present a different portrayal or a new truth about motherhood invites an obvious question: how do readers know that the lives narrated online are presented honestly? Can online life writing be trusted as an authentic representation of the lives being described?

Apart from a few well-documented hoaxes,[9] the veracity of online writing can be evidenced by the sheer numbers of bloggers who go on to encounter one another offline. Furthermore, since most bloggers exist within a dialogic and responsive space, they are as likely to be caught out in minor inconsistencies as people who tell routine falsehoods to their offline communities. At the same time, as authors, bloggers decide which stories to include or omit in their narratives, and which details to foreground. As many life writing theorists have addressed, the line between life writing and fiction is by no means a sturdy barrier. Furthermore, life writing acknowledges that no story is exclusively about its author; thus, while life writing is often written in first person, it includes third-person descriptions of the many people with whom the author's life intersects. It is precisely this focus on relationality and slippages that makes life writing so useful as a means of analysis for mommyblogs. The implications of this view of life writing move completely away from representations of autobiography as static truth, a unified and objective portrait of a subject, to something much more ambiguous and fruitful.

Smith and Watson (1998, 2001) use psychoanalytic and postmodern theories to open up the field of women's autobiography and consider these ambiguities, focusing on the ways that writing contributes to subject creation rather than merely documentation. Smith and Watson also take a view of women's life writing as contributing to collective subjectivities and alliances, arguing that "crucially, the writing and theorizing of women's lives has often occurred in texts that place an emphasis on collective processes while questioning the sovereignty and universality of the solitary self" (1998, p. 5). Such an analysis moves far beyond a reckoning of blogs as "true" or "false" and instead sees the supple interaction between author and writing as mutually constitutive. Nonetheless, the potential anonymity of blogs provokes frequent concerns by critics and media about their veracity. Some of these concerns might be born of the popular audience of blogs; distinct from critical memoirs read and reviewed by literary critics, blogs are often perceived as "casual" writing, as "simple" accounts of everyday life. If the purpose of blogging is merely to describe lived experiences, then issues of truth-telling may be foregrounded. To understand why these concerns are facile, the issue of authenticity in blogs must be taken up through the lenses of discourse and performativity. These lenses may be initially considered with respect to the disembodiment of blogging.

The major difference between on- and offline interactions is the extent to which the former allow for the body to remain absent from discourse. Offline, people may not be able to avoid their social location with respect to gender roles, race, and certain disabilities, to name but a few sites. By contrast, at least theoretically, people can construct online identities that do not reveal physical characteristics, allowing other attributes to be foregrounded. In practice, this erasure has both positive and negative consequences. On the one hand, bloggers with disabilities, for example, can transcend their physical bodies and present the aspects of themselves they see as central, rather than being defined by their disabilities. At the same time, the absence of the body tends to erase marginalized identities that are not specifically referenced, so that racialized bloggers who do not write about race, for example, are often assumed to be white.

Cyberspace presents a new form of performativity, one that allows subjects to emphasize aspects of identity that might be less noticeable in real life, while simultaneously minimizing physical identity markers.

Rather than focusing on whether life writing presents an empirical truth, then, it is instead useful to see this space as emblematic of a new form of performativity that allows for the self in creation and in response to cultural norms and strictures. Such an analysis, while not totally uninterested in the "truth" of women's lives online, acknowledges the limitations of truth in these accounts (particularly in light of their role as discursively constructed representations of social life, limited by both choice and lack thereof) and the reader's ability to discern such "truths." Rather than considering these blogs as static documents that present a fixed version of any given life, life writing theory (such as that of Smith & Watson, 1998) allows me to consider them as collages, mosaics in whose creation I may participate in order to begin to consider the experiences of mothers at the beginning of the twenty-first century.

In her consideration of performativity, Judith Butler (1993) posited that the markers of gender that are generally externally presented are the result of ongoing repetitive acts and language that entrench particular identities and positions as normal. Butler sought to understand the ways that gender is about power and control rather than nature and argued that the feminine or masculine subject was constructed through its adherence to a larger institutional system and the discourse it produced. She notes,

> At stake in such a reformulation of the materiality of bodies will be . . .
> the understanding of performativity not as the act by which a subject
> brings into being what she/he names, but, rather, as that reiterative power
> of discourse to produce the phenomena that it regulates and constrains.
> (p. 2)

In Butler's usage, performativity thus constitutes dominant discourse. She argues that "performativity is thus not a singular 'act,' for it is always a reiteration of a norm or a set of norms, and to the extent that it acquires an act-like status in the present, it conceals or dissimulates the conventions of which it is a repetition" (1993, p. 12). Butler's notion of performativity is a reminder that the individual subject and her actions are always occurring against the backdrop of a broader context. In considering performativity, however, Butler does not view individual subjects as puppets simply enacting scripts of dominance; neither does she consider individual subject positions politically neutral simply because they are performed rather than biologically inhabited. On the contrary: Butler presents performativity as a reminder that bodies *matter*, stating

that "the category of women does not become useless through deconstruction, but becomes one whose uses are no longer reified as 'refer-
ents' and which stand a chance of being opened up, indeed, of coming
to signify, in ways that none of us can predict in advance" (p. 29). If performativity describes our ability as mothers to create ourselves publicly
in the context of prescription and expectation, how is this performance
mediated at the intersection of maternity and technology? Cyberspace
changes the dynamics of performance, allowing for the possibility of a
counter-performance, one that challenges the "conventions of which it
is a repetition" and instead provides alternatives.

In following Butler's notions of performativity, I consider "women"
and "mothers" as constructed rather than biologically created, and as
unstable, incoherent subjects. Such an analysis thus moves beyond
potentially unhelpful concerns about truth-telling to consider the
ways that individual selves are presented and created. I will be considering what broader performative expectations are placed on mothers in order to constrain the choreography of modern motherhood but
will attempt to foreground the discursive and social implications of
this experience rather than seeing motherhood as stable, natural, or
otherwise fixed.

The Theoretical Frameworks

My preliminary analysis of the material showed an internal incoherence
in each of the sites and it was precisely this ambivalence and ambiguity
that I wanted to delve into most deeply. At the same time, it was of great
importance to me to adopt Donna Haraway's (1988) focus on a "network
of connections, including the ability partially to translate knowledges
among very different – and power-differentiated – communities" (p.
6). I wanted to foreground the interplay of power, identity, and diversity, especially in light of the historical lack of power accorded mothers,
as well as the obvious power imbalances among and between mothers over time and place. Simultaneously, however, I wanted to consider
power as (in Foucauldian terms) capillary and active, situated within
the discourses of a specific set of social practices, yet nonetheless providing moments of resistance, confusion, and possibility. Most of all, I
sought to respond to Shelley Park's (2010) concern that

the past two decades have witnessed the emergence of a rich body of feminist scholarship on mothering alongside an equally burgeoning body of

postmodernist scholarship on digital technologies and a rapidly prolifer-
ating and challenging body of literature in queer theory. However, there
has been little dialogue between feminists theorizing motherhood, on the
one hand, and cultural theorists . . . investigating the transgressive potential of our posthuman, postmodern condition, on the other hand. (p. 55)

In reading and analysing mommyblogs, I found that the liminality
and incoherence that I have come to cherish is best characterized by
three key terms: hybrid, cyborg, and queer. While all of these terms
have a variety of definitions and implications, I focus here on all three
as methods of resisting both stability and individuality in favour of a
more collective and disruptive means of analysis, yet one that still allows for a reckoning of the roles of power and privilege. It is precisely
the slipperiness and contested definitions of these three terms that led
me to borrow them, more for their possibilities than their answers, and
to see them as the defining focus of this project. I apply each of these
in the following chapters to look more deeply into the voices of the
mothers who are writing, to search out what they are saying and how
their writings are shifting definitions of motherhood. The terms, which
I define briefly here, will help elucidate more fully the complexities of
agency, power, identity, and subjectivity of motherhood.

Hybrid

I use the term "hybrid" to discuss the diversity of the mamasphere,
considering the ways that mothers' online life writing greatly extends
the range of possible maternal stories that a reader might access. Looking at mommyblogs, I am able to consider a breadth of experience from
an immense range of social locations generally excised or marginalized
from more traditional parenting texts. Likewise, non-normative family
formations and parenting practices are documented in detail in the mamasphere but are represented much more sparsely elsewhere.

In addition to this reading of hybridity as emblematic of social diversity, theories of hybridity allow for an analysis of the diverse and
unstable subject presented by any given mommyblogger: in the online
context where mothers are characterized by their multiplicity, there is
hybridity in each blogger as well as across the mamasphere as a whole.
An understanding of the hybrid draws heavily from theories of hybridity within life writing theory and feminist epistemology. Barbara
Bridger (2009) describes the convention of *écriture féminine*, women's

writing, as a form of hybridity present in life writing. Bridger suggests that

> écriture féminine was concerned with how language operates in relation to identity, how it "performs" the self, how it simultaneously reflects and creates. Its proponents looked for forms of writing capable of producing knowledge; writing engaged in the formation of the self; writing that observes the making of that self, but which cannot be, in the articulation of those observations, divorced from the self. (p. 340)

Mommyblogs borrow from and extend the tradition of écriture féminine by allowing for the formation of the self under observation from both within and beyond the individual doing the writing. Matthew Wilson (2009) extends this notion of hybrid self-creation and observation by considering the ontological implications of hybridity. He argues that "ontological hybridity is about contingent beings and about forms of becoming that challenge dualist narratives" (p. 499), positing that hybridity can become its own form of analysis. Wilson suggests that we require a "kind of working hybridity, where subjectivities are re-made in boundary crossings. Working hybrids invoke multiplicity, contingency and blurred, unraveling boundaries" (p. 503). Perhaps anticipating the relationality of the cyborg blogosphere, Wilson suggests that such a hybrid context allows for the relational dimensions of self-creation to emerge in the context of community, arguing that we have a responsibility to work towards "an ethic of making knowledges by working those hybrid encounters which place us at risk – to acquire one another in an enacting of responsible collaboration" (p. 506).

Cyborg

The term "cyborg" has allowed me to look closely at the dialogism of the Internet and the ways that this relational space has led to a burgeoning dialogue that is more consistent with the ways that mothers interact offline than the ways that texts have historically been organized.

In order to delve into the intricacies of online communication, it is important to consider the role of theoretical approaches to cyberspace, beginning with Haraway's (1985) "Cyborg Manifesto." Haraway narrates the melting of boundaries between human/machine and human/animal, locating in that disruption possibilities both "monstrous" and potentially redemptive (p. 155). Referring to "cybernetic organisms" or "cyborgs," Haraway takes care to avoid either valorizing or demonizing our emergent cyborg selves unduly; rather, she cautions that we must note both the ubiquity and potency of the cyborg. As our reliance on mediated technologies grows, they become invisible, "as hard to see politically as materially" (p. 153). Haraway asserts that the hybridity, fluidity, and essential non-*naturalness* of cyborgs may afford possibilities both dangerous and fruitful: "The main trouble with cyborgs, of course, is that they are the illegitimate offspring of militarism and patriarchal capitalism, not to mention state socialism. But illegitimate offspring are often exceedingly unfaithful to their origins. Their fathers, after all, are inessential" (p. 151). Yvonne Volkart (2004) credits Haraway with "the shift from feminism to cyberfeminism" (p. 99), noting that the tensions between corporeality and machinism and the chaos and excess of an increasingly technologically emergent existence have led to a feminist presence specifically concerned with these characteristics. Volkart argues that cyberfeminism takes on existing feminist notions of technology as specifically liberatory and expands on them, noting that "cyberfeminism promotes both the idea of becoming cyborgian and the pleasures involved in it. In other words, technologies are no longer perceived as prostheses and instruments for liberation which are separated from the body, but a merging of body and technology takes place" (p. 99). This blurring of body-machine boundaries can be seen in the "Cyberfeminist Manifesto," written by cyberfeminist art/activist collective VNS Matrix in 1991. The manifesto reads, in part,

> we are the virus of the new world disorder
> rupturing the symbolic from within
> saboteurs of big daddy mainframe
> the clitoris is a direct line to the matrix [. . .]
> infiltrating disrupting disseminating
> corrupting the discourse
> we are the future cunt[10]

This manifesto "reproduced itself virally" and was eventually translated into seven languages. In attempting to understand its significance, it is necessary to look at the interplay between body and machine language and the confusion and ambiguity of the text, as well as at its clear political rejection of "big daddy mainframe." In its unusual syntax, this manifesto also portrays a collective identity ("we are the future cunt") without foreclosing the possibilities of difference within its collective "subject." Thus, this document presents some of the possibilities of simultaneous connection/disruption, of an incoherent body linked with a chaotic machine as an extension (rather than a foreclosure) of radical possibilities.

Within cyberspace and cyberfeminism, the lines between representation and reality extend the blurring of a discursive approach to the social world. Anne Balsamo (1999) suggests, "In traveling through various virtual cyberworlds, it no longer makes sense to ask whose reality or perspective is *represented* in cyberspace; rather, we should ask what reality is created therein, and how this reality articulates relationships among technologies, bodies, and narratives" (p. 15). While initially this positioning of cyberculture may be viewed as technologically deterministic, I would like to argue that it is, in fact, simply an extension of existing discursive analyses that view social arrangements as simultaneously being constructed by and constructing discourse. To discuss the construction of the social world, however, may be a misrepresentation, characterizing the social as something tangible – like a building or a book – that has an internal order and a date for completion. Rather, this "construction" must be understood to be bi-directional, chaotic, ongoing, and fragmented. Furthermore, while acknowledging the impact of cyberspace on cultural mediation and creation, all cybercreation is still nonetheless constrained by existing discourses that privilege hegemonic and patriarchal power arrangements. This returns us to the self-consciousness that Haraway requires; left unacknowledged, cyberspace may indeed replicate the frontier, with all the colonialist implications that this analogy may summon. The cyberworld, however, is no more *terra nulla* than the ground on which we as humans stand, and in order to credibly understand its impact, cyberspace must be considered within the existing social and cultural discourses, even as they emerge, respond, and mutate in response to machines. Haraway (1985) cautions that "our machines are disturbingly lively, and we ourselves frighteningly inert" (p. 152). Only by enlivening our "selves" can we usefully begin to consider the existing constraints on the cyborg as a point of resistance.

Queer

Drawing from both postmodernism and feminist theory, queer theory begins with the term "queer" itself as an act of resistance to the growing acronym – GLBT and other additions – by seeing these terms as both totalizing and limiting to the full range of human experiences. While "queer" itself refers to shifts in non-normative identity with respect to sexuality and gender, queer theory takes these insights and applies them to subject formation more broadly. David Halperin (1997) writes, "Queer is by definition whatever is at odds with the normal, the legitimate, the dominant. There is nothing in particular to which it necessarily refers. It is an identity without an essence. 'Queer' then, demarcates not a positivity but a positionality vis-à-vis the normative" (p. 62).

Important to any study of maternity is queer theory's resistance to any essential or natural component of identity. Rather, identity is viewed as discursively constructed and performed and thus in flux. While the roots of this theory sought to respond to debates around the essential nature of homosexuality, these insights are interestingly applied to the realm of motherhood where similarly normative ideals are often put forth, and to complementary realms such as family, femininity, and reproduction. Likewise, queer theory posits the slipperiness of language as an ever-evolving terrain, viewing language as a space that potentially limits the possibilities of subjects by concretizing human experience into overly rigid boxes. Again, with respect to motherhood, the application of these insights bears relevance, as motherhood is a terrain that is both prescriptive and highly organized by language – to speak of mothers is, for example, most of the time to speak of women, despite the considerable gender variation in people who mother. William Turner (2000) writes, "One vastly oversimplified but still useful way to understand queer theory begins with the proposition that many persons do not fit the available categories and that such a failure of fit reflects a problem not with the persons but with the categories" (p. 32).

Critics of queer theory argue that the fluidity of the theory allows for an ignorance of the material conditions that organize social relations. Its proponents, by contrast, suggest that the realities of social relations are misrepresented by an overly rigid adherence to apocryphal identity categories. Eve Kosofsky Sedgwick (1991) argues,

> A tiny number of inconceivably coarse axes of categorization have been painstakingly inscribed in current critical and political thought: gender, race, class, nationality, sexual orientation are pretty much the available distinctions. They, with the associated demonstrations of the mechanisms by which they are constructed and reproduced, are indispensable, and they may indeed override all or some other forms of difference and similarity. But the sister or brother, the best friend, the classmate, the parent,

the child, the lover, the ex-: our families, work, play, and activism, prove that even people who share all or most of our positions along these crude axes may still be different enough from us, and from each other, to seem like all but different species. (p. 22)

Sedgwick asks us to reject these "crude axes" and instead to consider our hybridity and variegation, the ways we perform and are performed upon to arrive at more nuanced and less rigid conclusions.

Hybrid, cyborg, and queer each have a long history and cover important theoretical terrain, yet each concept is also open to interpretation and mixed understandings. Collectively, these terms allow for the maternal subject to emerge in an ambiguous and exciting way. These terms position blogging within life writing as a space that resists the fixity of selfhood in favour of more nuanced readings of subjectivity that challenge the status quo.

About This Book

I aim to build a case for the presence of mommyblogs as innovative forms of maternal life writing that, taken collectively, begin to shift understandings of maternal subjectivity by presenting a public and multitudinous account of many mothers' practices. Only by considering the ways that writing on maternity has shifted and grown – and the emergence of new and dominant discourses of motherhood – can this trend or the implications of its widespread popularity be understood.

The remainder of this book will suggest that the major characteristics of mommyblogs – their diversity and dialogism – result in a collective response to dominant discourses of motherhood. This response privileges the voices of many mothers, and the connections between them, over the limited stories historically told about mothers. Chapter 2 will foreground this discussion by considering the history of the mamasphere and of blogging practice more generally, while the remaining chapters will use the theoretical foundations to interrogate the major attributes of the mamasphere. Chapter 3 will focus on the hybridity and richness of individual accounts as well as the diversity of marginalized social locations and parenting practices seen in mommyblogging. Chapter 4 will consider the creation of community and dialogue through the dynamism of mommyblogs as inherently social. Chapter 5 will consider whether the unique traits of mommyblogs can shift a perception of the maternal subject beyond rigid constructions of motherhood towards a more complicated and manifold maternal sub-jectivity. Finally, the conclusion will consider the precariousness of this medium and the shifts already posed by emerging technologies.

2   A Short History of the Mamasphere and the Discursive Construction of Motherhood

I vividly remember feeling monitored when I was visibly pregnant. Feeling as though I'd get in trouble when I bought wine for cooking or beer for a party, or smelled or tried a sip of my partner's drink when we were out. And multiple baristas actually did try to correct me when I ordered various sorts of tea ("oh, that has caffeine; we have xyz herbal teas") . . . let alone espresso. They gave up in the face of the Look of Death, as my mother calls it, but they still simultaneously pissed me off and made me feel small. (Even though the whole problem was that I was so big.) I've never as an adult felt so *watched*, so much under societal observance and – potentially – discipline.

— Molly Westerman, *Feminist Childbirth Studies*[1]

Mommyblogging, as a practice, has shifted understandings of motherhood. To best understand the roots of this shift, it is necessary to look to the history of blogging itself as well as the ways that motherhood came to be seen as a unique and definitive criterion for bloggers. How did personal online life writing become such a central component of daily communication in the industrialized world? Within this emergent genre, how did motherhood become such an important and commodified space, and one that so completely defined its authors? An examination of blogging practice provides the background for the history of the mamasphere and will allow for an understanding of the specific methods – critical discourse analysis informed by life writing theory – that guide this book.

How Blogging Happens

Technorati, the world's largest blog aggregating tool, argues that "blogs are pervasive and part of our daily lives."[2] According to NM Incite, a subsidiary of Neilson Industries, as of December 2011 there were over

181 million public blogs in existence.[3] While there is no way to measure how many of the blogs that are started nearly immediately become defunct, blogging is clearly not the domain of a prolific few. Shel Israel notes that "until recently, 'the Blogosphere' referred to a small cluster of geeks circled around a single tool. Now it refers to hundreds of millions of people using a vast warehouse of tools that allow people to behave increasingly online like they do in real life. We have entered the Age of Normalization in the Blogosphere."[4] Yet apart from the stable characteristics of blogs – reverse-chronological dated entries and interactive links – do weblogs have coherent generic components?

Miller and Shepherd (2009) contend, "With a rapidity equal to that of their initial adoption, blogs became not a single discursive phenomenon but a multiplicity" (p. 263). Even as blogs are characterized by their breadth and diversity, the emotional interactions between bloggers and readers (often, though not always, who are bloggers themselves) are essential characteristics of blogging practice. This practice, Jill Walker Rettberg suggests, has shifted our culture. Walker Rettberg (2008) argues that "we have moved from a culture dominated by mass media, using one-to-many communication, to one where participatory media, using many-to-many communication, is becoming the norm" (p. 31).

For most casual Internet users, blogs have come to be understood as relatively personal accounts of bloggers' lives and surroundings for an online audience. What tends to characterize a blog in the popular imagination is a sense that the personality of the author emerges through more than necessarily factual information about her or his life. Blogs allow access to the voice of a person, albeit in a highly mediated way. As Aaron Barlow (2008) insists, "If the blogs are changing our culture, it is because of the individual bloggers, not because of the other uses that have been found for the blogs, no matter how fascinating these may prove to be" (p. x). Barlow notes that personal blogs have made technology more intimate and have emphasized the personal over the corporate in heretofore unrealized ways.

To some extent, the revolutionary potential of blogs is found in a shift away from more traditional journalistic principles of objectivity, replaced instead by the insistence on an authorial stance, replete with biases and subjectivities. *Time* magazine, reporting in 2004, noted that "blogs don't pretend to be neutral: they're gleefully, unabashedly biased, and that makes them a lot more fun" (Grossman & Hamilton, 2004, para. 9).

Personal authorship allows a relatively high degree of autonomy thus far unrealized in any other medium – a deeply public space in which one may share private thoughts, or just muse on breakfast cereals, reality TV shows, or political scandal. Whether the content is useful is a question that is both loaded and unprofitable. Barlow (2008) insists, "A blog is only as boring as any piece of writing" (p. xiii). What is clear is that personal blogs have allowed an extraordinary range of "normal" people to share their ideas with a potentially limitless audience. This audience is likewise potentially drawn in by the mundanity, rather than the exceptionality, of the writing. Blog readers responding to a survey undertaken by Karlsson (2006) "do not speak of seeking the exceptional and the strange. Rather, they speak of seeking and being comforted by reading the prosaic relations of people like them" (p. 3).

As McNeill (2003) suggests, "In their immediacy and accessibility in their seemingly unmediated state, Web diaries blur the distinction between online and offline lives, 'virtual reality' and 'real life,' 'public' and 'private,' and most intriguingly for auto/biography studies, between the life and the text" (p. 25). Yet to imply that this personal authorship allows unbounded self-communication online dismisses the other important characteristic of present-day bloggers: their participation in the blogosphere and its relationality. Bloggers only have an audience, for the most part, if they link up with other blog sites and comment on other authors' blogs. The result is a uniquely collective authorship that creates a narrative that extends across multiple online spaces. Gurak, Antonijevic, Johnson, Ratliff, and Reyman (2004) argue that

> we find value in the power of blogs to forego the institutionalization of communicative practices and offer spaces for writing that are more collaboratively constructed than other online spaces, as bloggers freely link to, comment on, and augment each other's content. In this way, blogs allow for the possibility of developing new cultural practices of online communication in relation to previously established modes of ownership, authorship, and legitimacy of content and access to information. (para. 1)

This function, the creation of an actual web of links into an ongoing snarled and multidimensional conversation, mediates the content of each and every blog. Blogs are *not* simply the private musings of individuals, made public. Rather, they are a form of participation in a vast and never-ending conversation. Herve Fischer (2006) makes this point explicitly, arguing that "the deluge of individual blogs about anything is astonishing, expressing a vertiginous desire for communication" (p. 64). Fischer's point, foregrounding communication over narrative, is exceedingly important as a response to those who point to blogs as a self-aggrandizing form of solipsism. This claim ignores the passionate desire to communicate that informs many blogs, that has led to the development, not of infinite blogging islands, but of a vast, relational blogosphere. As Michael Bérubé (2006) notes,

> The best, most thought-provoking blogs are renowned not only for the quality of their writing, but for the quality of writing they stimulate in response. It is in the daily give-and-take between bloggers and commenters – many of whom, of course, have their own blogs as well – that discursive communities are formed online, and it is in such give-and-take that blogs create the taste by which they are to be enjoyed. (p. 289)

To discuss the blogosphere as though it were one stable entity does not adequately convey the many different and convergent areas of this cyberzone. While there is a focus on the blogosphere, then, as "a medium in which people are expected to and do engage directly, thus extending the discursive boundary outside of the hyperreal and into every possible aspect of the blogger's life" (Harden, 2009, p. 254), blogging connections do not tend to totalize social location and identity in the ways towards which real-life affinity groups have, at their worst, tended (Karlsson, 2006, p. 9). The sheer speed of the Internet, the ability to connect with hundreds of people sharing different affinities in a matter of moments, thus causes intense connection simultaneous with intense multiplicity. To talk of "the blogosphere" or "multiple blogospheres" is to run headlong into the limitations of language in order to convey the flexibility and mutability of spaces online. Keeping this caveat in mind, however, I now turn briefly to an examination of the history and composition of the mamasphere.

Creation of the Mamasphere

The emergence of "mommyblogger" as an online identity occurred alongside all the controversy that such niches tend to create. Facing criticism from journalists and other bloggers, mommybloggers emerged as a group who had to fight hard to be taken seriously, and who were both defiant and committed to their writing. Two major events helped "mommyblogger" cohere into a public identity and established the mamasphere (sometimes spelled "momosphere") as an emergent cyber-landscape of maternal community, activism, and discussion.

Writing in the *New York Times*, David Hochman (2005, January) sought to chronicle the emergence of a new style of blog written by parents about parenting and children, noting that "there is not a tale from the crib (no matter how mundane or scatological) that is unworthy of narration . . . The baby blog in many cases is an online shrine to parental self-absorption" (para. 2). While the piece never used the word "mommyblogger" and interviewed, among many mothers, one father who was blogging about parenthood, it was nonetheless clearly a piece about maternal solipsism as evidenced by the title: "Mommy (and me)." The article echoed concerns emerging within the blogosphere about the appropriateness of motherhood as a source of "blog fodder," centring on two key concerns: the privacy of children being documented by their mothers online, and the perceived boringness of maternal accounts. While these criticisms of women who blogged about family had been emergent for several years, Hochman's article reified these critiques and thus inflamed the women who were about to be called mommybloggers. Across the then nascent mamasphere, women angrily responded. As Eden Marriott Kennedy of *Fussy* wrote, "Good morning, I'm humorless and resentful, as are many moms who blog. We overscrutinize our children's every excretion and whore out adorable anecdotes about them just to get attention for ourselves!"[5] Kyra of *This Mom* responded to Hochman's assertion that mothers blog for validation by arguing, "I don't think people are blogging to *get* validation. People are blogging to save their sanity, to give *themselves* attention and validation. In fact, I think this generation of parents is *less* in need of validation and much more willing to stand up and say, this is how it looks over here and I'm writing it down. If you're interested, come have a peek."[6]

While Hochman's article sought to diminish the validity of maternal online life writing, it instead galvanized defiant responses and potentially led to the ironic reclamation of "mommyblogger" as an identity category. Just like any other bloggers, "mothers who blogged" generally covered a range of topics. By focusing on writing about the day-to-day realities of motherhood, however, mommyblogging emerged as a specific niche and mommybloggers as particular players within the larger blogosphere. While women who blogged about their children might not have changed their conventions and still focused on multiple topics, they were nonetheless increasingly defined, after Hochman's article, as women who blogged about motherhood. This shift set the stage for the further entrenchment of "mommyblogging" as a practice, which took hold later that same year.

In the summer of 2005, a blogging site by the name of *BlogHer* ("the community for women who blog") hosted its first conference in response to a perceived ghettoization of women within the blogosphere. The three *BlogHer* cofounders, Elisa Camahort Page, Jory Des Jardins, and Lisa Stone, began this three-hundred-person conference by attempting to answer the question "Where are the women bloggers?"[7] The conference, held in San Jose, California, brought together blogging women from a wide range of backgrounds and interests, many of whom had technical or political backgrounds that allowed them to capitalize on the resource of blogging for professional, rather than simply personal, gain. There were relatively few women who kept blogs detailing maternal and family narratives at the conference. Lori Kido Lopez (2009) notes, "It quickly became clear that women who wrote about their children were not allowed into the discussions carried on by other women in the blogosphere – other women who wrote about things such as technology and current events" (p. 736).

In response, these women were given their own panel. As Jenn of *Mommy Needs Coffee* wrote later, "We were told it would be a small room and not to feel bad as it may not have many attendees. In fact, I believe the words 'mommyblogging' and 'passing phase' were used by Elisa."[8]

The panel on mommyblogging centred on the word itself, asking whether it demeaned both those to whom the term applied and women bloggers more broadly, and whether mommybloggers were letting down their "serious" sisters by chronicling such stereotypically female domains. More importantly, confounding expectations to the contrary, "the room was filled to capacity. Not only were other mom bloggers present, but tech bloggers, literary agents, a reporter and others who were just curious to see what we had to say."[9] Despite the interest, mommybloggers were still perceived as dilettantes who detracted from the more serious female voices online. To cap the growing tension, at the closing keynote a conference attendee remarked to the mommybloggers that if they "stopped blogging about themselves, they could change the world." At this, blogger Alice Bradley stood and stated, "Mommyblogging is a radical act."[10] Jenn expands on Alice's comment with the benefit of hindsight:

At that time, to be called a mommyblogger and have a mommyblog was radical. We had to fight for any respect we received. We had to work hard to earn any recognition that was not negative. It was radical to embrace (or even accept) being called a mommyblogger.

What did we walk away with that day? If "they" were going to continue to label us mommybloggers, we would make it a term that was synonymous with respect, integrity and quality writing. The opinions and writing styles represented by the women in that room at that panel were as varied as the writers behind them. It wasn't as if we walked away holding hands and singing "Kumbaya." We weren't suddenly some bonded community that adored each other and created a uniform way of mommyblogging. For goodness sakes, some of us didn't even like each other but we did respect the writing represented by each one of us.

Regardless of any of our differences, we did agree on one thing: We would no longer sit back and be disrespected for being a mommyblogger. We were not going to sit at the bottom rung of the blogging ladder and be content. As a collective of individual writers, we were taking back the term and demanding respect. Not by telling people to respect us. Not by storming the gates of the media and demand[ing] they respect us. No, we gained respect through our writing. Call us what you want – label us what you want – we were first and foremost writers. Good writers. We just happened to write about our family lives and our children.[11]

While the controversy surrounding the 2005 BlogHer conference certainly galvanized many mommybloggers into defiantly refusing to be dismissed or undermined by external perspectives on maternal narrative, the conference also took advantage of personal connections between bloggers. Lopez (2009) found that following the controversy, bloggers responding to the panel sought validation and solidarity from blogging about motherhood, despite their frustrations with the evident belittlement of being reduced to "mommies" (p. 236). By providing a space for many mommybloggers to connect with one another and ally against the discrimination they faced at the conference, BlogHer 2005 arguably stabilized the mamasphere into its own corner of the Internet, albeit a corner with shifting and unstable boundaries.

If Hochman firmly entrenched "mommyblogger" into the lexicon, then BlogHer 2005 arguably provided the mamasphere as a way of describing the organic interconnectedness of blogging mothers, both on- and offline. This interconnectedness has had powerful effects.

Lisa Hammond (2010) documented how mommyblogging has shifted the cultural understanding of motherhood, arguing that "women blogging about mothering and those who read these women's blogs contribute to the multiplicity of voices developing new cultural definitions of motherhood, definitions that are both individual and distinct but also communal in nature, a collective memory through which women rewrite the roles of mothering in contemporary culture" (p. 86). By critically examining the writing of a large sample of mommyblogs, this book will consider these collectively authored shifts and the ways they may challenge existing patriarchal views of motherhood and maternal identity.

How Are Mommyblogs Read?

If the mamasphere is, as argued above, characterized by both diversity and dialogue, how can it be successfully analysed? As Susan Herring (2010) argues,

> The full extent of the blogosphere is nearly as unmeasurable as that for the web as a whole, given the high rate of churn in blog creation and abandonment, the existence of private blogs, the presumed high number of blogs in other languages hosted by services that are not indexed by English-language search engines, and so forth; this makes random sampling of the blogosphere a practical impossibility. (p. 244)

Keeping in mind Herring's warning, I undertook an analysis of more than two hundred mommyblogs. The process of selecting the blogs for this project evolved over time and followed a nonlinear path. Part grounded theory, part treasure hunt, the selection was provocative and challenging. The limitations of examining the Internet, or even, to narrow it down, the millions of blogs that comprise the mamasphere, lead to questions about the need for shifts in research design to accommodate this vast terrain.

I began by randomly selecting blogs from *BlogHer*'s list of Mommy and Family Blogs in order to get a sense of the range of "average" mommyblogs selected solely by chance. These blogs were read relatively cursorily, often by looking at twenty to thirty posts or two to three months of archive. In order to consider questions of diversity and identity, however, I then handpicked a large number of mommyblogs that represented diverse social locations, maternal identities, parenting practices, or family compositions. Finally, in order to understand the phenomenon of mommyblogging more completely, I deliberately selected four highly popular mommyblogs (*Dooce, Finslippy, Fussy,* and *Her Bad Mother*). In the case of hand-picked and popular blogs, I read the majority of a blog's archive. For all blogs, however, to understand the interconnectivity of the mamasphere and the creation of community among mommybloggers, I read outgoing links and comments on most blogs and often added new blogs to the study through links from selected blogs. I thus read the mamasphere as a linked and interactive web, rather than as a disparate list of narratives. I considered Jill Walker Rettburg's (2008) suggestion that "the best way to understand blogging is to immerse yourself in it" (p. 1).

Once I selected the sample of blogs for this research, I began to read. Guided by theories of life writing, I undertook a critical discourse analysis of the blogs, both singly and collectively. Critical discourse analysis (CDA) is necessarily selective and therefore well suited to an undertaking as vast as an examination of the web. As van Dijk (2001) notes, "In any practical sense, there is no such thing as a 'complete' discourse analysis: a 'full' analysis of a short passage might take months and fill hundreds of pages. Complete discourse analysis of a large corpus of text or talk, is therefore totally out of the question" (p. 99). Far from being a failing of this approach, however, the candidness with which CDA approaches its selectivity is potentially one of its strengths. CDA is a specifically political perspective, one that seeks to map out and shed light on the pathways of power abuse and domination, and to provide a context for discussion of the discursive implications of hegemonic social structures for traditionally underrepresented social players (Naples, 2003). It is, van Dijk argues, "discourse analysis, 'with an attitude'" (p. 96).

My analysis began by considering the implications of discourse and the ways that life writing allows for the creation of identity through discourse. Looking at the discursive construction of motherhood through these life writing texts allowed me to consider complex issues of power and agency that led me to my final analytical grounding in the realms of hybrid, cyborg, and queer theory.

Discourse

Within a postmodern framework, discourse is viewed as comprising the building blocks of the social world. While discussion of discourse is sometimes limited to analysis of conversation and text, generally discourse is more broadly understood to acknowledge spoken word, gesture, dress, and other sensory information deliberately or tacitly conveyed between people. In Foucault's terms, discourse so irreparably mediates all social interactions that a discussion of objective truth "beneath" discourse is rendered moot – any and all information can only be accessed by resorting to discourse and thus cannot ever know what is beyond this sphere.

In some respects, to discuss discourse and maternity in the context of mommyblogs is simply facile: blogs themselves are, arguably, wholly discursive. As Deborah Bowen (2009) writes,

> Within these online diary sites, women can appropriate and manipulate language into an entirely female discourse. Certainly, the women who diary online are creating the strictest, most literal definition of autobiography; women who publish online are engaging in the formulation of thoughts and ideas, a free reflexive exchange between Self and Self, creating (writing!) herself as she keys in her words. (p. 312)

Obviously, the content of every blog is completely mediated through the lens of its author(s). Thus, to discuss motherhood and social relations in the context of blogs by looking at discourse is both an obvious and a superficial choice. To consider the choices made by authors as discursive agents might be interesting, but would not, in isolation, provide the critical analysis that typifies feminist scholarship at its best. It is the introduction of an analysis of power, and of a specific element of *critical* analysis, then, that is required in order to provide a fruitful investigation. While as a feminist scholar I would argue that critical analysis is required in all fields, it is especially important, and especially compelling, when looking at the power relations of mothers to their partners, to their communities, to their children, and to their own social identity and subjective construction of self.

Power

This book undertakes a poststructuralist approach to power, withdrawing from a reckoning of power that is commodifiable, something that may be held or taken away like a three-dimensional object. In this approach, mothers can't be said to be powerless or, indeed, powerful. Neither is power itself viewed as negative, as, in the words of Michel

Foucault (1980) himself, "power would be a fragile thing if its only function were to repress" (p. 59). A capillary view of power that sees it as an omnipresent practice of social relations makes a great deal of sense in looking at the situation of many contemporary mothers. Mothers might experience barriers to power in many respects, yet they hold extraordinary power in others: mothers hold a great deal of power over their children, literally, to use Foucault's (1991) term, *governing* them, "reckon[ing] with all the possible events that may intervene" (p. 94). A view of power that correlates power with oppression does not provide a satisfactory understanding of the complex power relations within families. Likewise, however, mothers must be seen to enact their power in the private sphere under the constraint of significant discursive constructions that limit, warp, or otherwise manipulate the experience of that power.

By way of example: a mother may insist that her child practice the piano in anticipation of his lesson, yet the experience of that moment of power holds shadows of other discourses: of the mother potentially responding to the mores of her community; of her own unrealized desire to have learned an instrument in her childhood; and, indeed, of her genuine wish to open her child's mind to musicality and to ensure that he is afforded possibilities for advancement within a society that privileges certain types of culture. Thus, maternal power is not only enacted but also simultaneously mediated – both by other discourses and through the relationship between mother and child – potentially endlessly. In addition, mothers may enact power in the public sphere in order to respond to a lack of power in the private sphere; the reverse may equally be true.

Patriarchal motherhood might itself be seen as a form of *biopower*, as described by Foucault: the simultaneous regulation of body and population. One must wonder if subsequent volumes of *The History of Sexuality* (1976), had they appeared, would have considered the ways that maternal bodies are controlled as a means of population control. The flow of power is once again disrupted, however, as mothers themselves may provide the earliest instances of regulation of children's sexuality. Foucault (1976) writes,

Biopower was without question an indispensable element in the development of capitalism; the latter would not have been possible without the controlled insertion of bodies into the machinery of production and the adjustment of the phenomena of population to economic processes. But this was not all it required; it also needed the growth of both these factors, their reinforcement as well as their availability and docility; it had to have methods of power capable of optimizing forces, aptitudes and life in general without at the same time making them more difficult to govern. (pp. 140–1)

Foucault considers biopower in relation to sexuality and reproduction but does not delve deeply into control over the cultivation of population in the form of mothering. As a result, a complicated moment of power is missed as mothers can be seen to be both controlled by, and making use of, biopower. In reinforcing the regulation of their children's bodies mothers exercise power, yet even the demand that small bodies avoid unruliness comes from a larger relationship of power that, at its source, is intrinsic to patriarchal motherhood and must be considered in relation to other sites of oppression.

Inside the discourses of the blogosphere, power is questioned, altered, and diffused through text – the experience of an individual mother is constantly mediated by the expectations of her audience, or the need for monetary or social advancement. The blogosphere itself may serve to undermine or subvert classical discourses and in this respect might be conceived of as a "heterotopia," a place where alternatives may flourish; it may, of course, simply reify existing discourses. In either case, however, beginning with a view of power that is broader than simply seeing it as a commodity allows for a more nuanced analysis. An examination of power, discourse, and maternity as a triad, with interconnections and flow between all three elements in all directions, thus leads to potentially interesting conclusions for all three individual elements. This particular line of inquiry leads squarely to critical discourse analysis as a method of approaching mommyblogs.

Critical discourse analysis aims to look at all forms of discourse as a recontextualization of social practices (van Leeuwan, 2008, p. 5). What makes critical discourse *critical*, however, is its emphasis on the way that power is held and lived through, and its specific focus on discourse as a "site of struggle, where forces of social (re)production and contestation are played out" (Lazar, 2005, p. 4). In providing an analysis of these forces, CDA aims to provide a "sophisticated theorization of the relationship between social practices and discourse structures" (Lazar, 2005, p. 4). Ruth Wodak and Michael Meyer (2001) further stress the historical and contextual nature of discourse as well as the interconnections between discourses, an emphasis that is of critical importance

in the particular analysis of the World Wide Web. By using critical discourse analysis as a means of reading mommyblogs, the thoughtful-
ness of these lives written into being is highlighted. Mommyblogs can
thus be considered as specific discursive constructions that emerge as
important forms of life writing and, in so doing, greatly intensify mul-
tiplicitous understanding of motherhood.

Life Writing Theory: The "Self-in-the-Writing"

A critical discourse analysis of mommyblogs is well served by being
grounded in life writing theory. Within this theory, life writing emerges
as a critical practice, one that allows "the reader to a) develop and foster
his/her own self-consciousness in order to b) humanize and make less
abstract (which is not to say less mysterious) the self-in-the-writing"
(Kadar, 1992, p. 12). Life writing itself is seen as "unfixed," as are both
its readers and its authors. As a lifelong reader of life writing, I feel myself implicated in the texts I read. I am drawn into other people's stories
and see the ways that such stories may change my own story as well as
the way that I tell it. As Karlsson (2006) offers, "the diary weblog . . . is a
mode of reading as much as it is a mode of writing" (p. 3). Life writing
theory thus helps me undertake an examination of texts as they "live at
the blurred edges of these questions of 'I' and 'we' and 'they'" (Kadar,
Warley, Perreault, & Egan, 2005, p. 5). Such an analysis has profound
implications for the examination of cyberspace where it is precisely the
connections between "authors" that may provide the most insight. Expanding on the methods afforded by CDA, then, the insights offered
by life writing theory provided a context to examine the connections,
instabilities, and inconsistencies in mothers writing online. Such an approach follows on the thinking of Paul John Eakin (1999) who suggests
that "*all* identity is relational, and that the definition of autobiography,
and its history as well, must be stretched to reflect the kinds of self-
writing in which relational identity is characteristically displayed" (p.
44). To do so is, to quote Kadar (1993), to finally learn to "read 'better.'
'Reading better' may be reading *for* contradiction, not against it" (p. xi).
  Yet even as I look at mommyblogs as discursively constructed, unstable, and ambiguous, I intend to heed the words of Laurie Finke (1992),
who argues,

  While recognizing the persuasiveness of poststructuralist theories of
  the sign which hold that the signified is endlessly deferred through the

disruptive free play of signifiers and that such disruption is potentially subversive of structures of order (including gender), theorists of cultural work also examine those hegemonic practices that create the illusion of a center that closes off this free play – practices that create the illusion of fixed meanings. (p. 193)

Writing the Life of the Mother

Mommyblogs present an interesting blend of a variety of forms of life writing. They are temporally unbounded and arranged chronologically, and are generally composed of a series of discrete entries; in this respect they most closely resemble diaries; indeed, the proto-blogs which preceded the rise of the blogosphere were understood to be online diaries. In their range and general lack of explicit focus or narrative arc, blogs are most consistent with journals or diaries that are written over time and are thus unfixed. Yet the terminology of "online diaries" foundered for a reason, since there are significant differences between blogs and diaries. While some diaries have always been intended for either sharing or publication, the majority of diaries have been private documents, at least within the lifetime of their author. Even public diaries tended to lack the dialogism that characterizes blogs generally and mommyblogs in particular. While diary cycles and other shared diary formats did begin to approach the relationality of the blogosphere, they still drew upon a limited pool of readers and writers and more closely resemble shared blogs than the sole-authored multiple dialogues that characterize most present-day blogs.

The relationality of the blogosphere, to be explored in greater detail in chapter 4, leads to an understanding of blogs as epistolary, rather than diaristic. Indeed, blogs can be understood as a convoluted web of writing and response that draws on the roots of letter writing as a consistent practice that is neither sole-authored nor entirely polyvocal; rather, letters and blogs allow for individual voices to participate in the creation of a shared story in which disagreement and contradiction are possible. The sheer speed and scope of the blogosphere, however, shift the epistolary nature of blogging; while an avid letter writer of the eighteenth or nineteenth century might have had dozens of correspondents, today's blogger might have hundreds or thousands of followers, as well as multiple fleeting interactions with commenters on their blogs or as commenters on others' blogs. Perhaps of most importance, however, is the immediacy of the Internet as a medium that assures responses in real time – this characteristic changes not only the scope of exchange but also its very nature, in that the style of writing that emerges is changed by its constancy. Karlsson (2007) argues that "the temporal proximity in the production/consumption of blogs reinforces the autobiographical contract online" (p. 147). Furthermore, writing on the Internet, characterized by Daniel Chandler (1998) as "much more *dynamic* than print" ("Asynchronous mass communication," para. 4), allows for a multisensory interactivity that is quite distinct from most earlier life writing formats. By the same token, online writing "disrupts notions of the materiality so vital to the traditional hand-held diary" (Podnieks, 2004, p. 129). Thus blogging emerges as a new form of life writing, but one with roots in early textual forms.

Blogging's unique characteristics have specific implications for mothers. As Linda Warley (2005) reminds us, "Online publishing encourages more people to make texts out of their [life stories] precisely because the publishing and marketing institutions are no longer serving as exclusive gatekeepers" (p. 27). This is critically important for mothers for whom stories of the private sphere have remained obscure and undiscussed. Self-publishing has allowed private women to own their stories, to respond to the absence of much maternal life and literary writing. As Elizabeth Podnieks and Andrea O'Reilly (2010) argue,

> Not only has the mother been lost to the broader traditions of literary history that have privileged narratives by and about male figures, but also she has been lost within the daughter-centric literatures that do depict the mother: she is absent to her children (almost always daughters) and to her self in that her own voice is silent, her subjectivity lacking or erased. (p. 12)

While Podnieks and O'Reilly's text begins to expose the maternal texts that exist within life writing, they nonetheless expose the historical absence of matrifocal narratives. By blogging, an array of mothers have been able to respond to that absence and reclaim their own voices; in an increasingly child-centred society, mothers online are able to tell their stories without waiting for a formal context in which to do so. As Aimee Morrison (2010) argues, "Personal mommy blogging is purposive and deliberate social engagement, a creative as well as interpersonal practice that mitigates the assorted ills (physical isolation, role confusion, lack of realistic role models, etc.) and celebrates the particular joys of contemporary mothering, especially in the earliest years of parenting" (para. 1). By creating a composite maternal narrative, furthermore, the mamasphere has exposed the great thirst that exists for mothers' stories, as evidenced by their explosive growth.

Lopez (2009) argues that "the self that emerges from a blog is neither cohesive nor singular, but instead determined through an amalgamation of conflicting elements" (p. 738). Critical discourse analysis and life writing theory allow for an examination that begins to examine the "conflicting elements" that are represented within mommyblogs, as both artefacts and community interactions. The remainder of this book will use poststructuralist theories of hybridity, cyborg, and queer theory to unpack the mamasphere and examine this dynamic space. In so doing, the book will show the ways that mommyblogging has led to an emergent shift in the story of motherhood, replacing expert discourse *about* mothers with intimate dialogue by and between them.

3 On Hybridity: The Diversity and Multiplicity of the Mamasphere

The reality is, none of us can paint an entirely clear picture of the reality of motherhood, because the reality of motherhood defies tidy characterization. Which is why, arguably, we see so much cultural discourse about motherhood that skews strongly in one direction or the other: we are constantly trying to get our bearings, and sometimes it's just easier to do so by telling ourselves that *motherhood is just so undeniably all-around awesome* or that *holy hell this shit is HARD* and sticking to those stories. And yes, those stories that skew dark are frightening, but then, so much of motherhood is frightening, notwithstanding the moments – and there are many – of awesome, so.

– Catherine Connor, *Her Bad Mother*[1]

Why care about mommyblogs? Having established the large number of mothers blogging, what is it about their stories that is unique and disruptive?

The mommyblogs I have read have been written by mothers who range from ages sixteen to seventy and up; who self-identify across the spectrum of race, including many mothers with hybridized racial identities; who represent a wide range of sexualities and gender positions; and who have a range of different abilities. Many mothers live at the intersections of these various identity markers, and blend these identities with other characteristics, such as identifying predominantly as abuse survivors or activists. In addition, mommyblogs, as self-authored documents, often highlight different aspects of identity than those that might be considered in looking at any individual mother from the outside in – a mommyblogger might believe that her experiences as a lawyer define her more completely than her position as a woman of colour, but this may not be the first identity marker that would characterize her in a physical environment. There is thus a complex relationship between identity, self-authorship, and dominant discourse taking place in all blogs, but especially for mothers wherein motherhood as an often totalizing identity marker is interspersed with the characteristics described above.

By using hybridity to unpack the mamasphere, it is possible to consider the diversity of maternal experiences and demographic spaces that are being recorded, as well as the ways that each blogger is presented as a rich and variegated character. A hybrid lens allows for the interruption of patriarchal tropes of motherhood, replacing them with a greater degree of heterogeneity and confusion. Such an interruption is sorely required as an antidote to the essentializing and minimizing rhetoric around motherhood elsewhere.

Like the blogs themselves, hybridity does not provide a conclusive lens. Rather, a hybrid lens allows a nuanced examination of the grey areas and contradictions of motherhood and of the maternal subject that focuses on diversity and multiplicity, the two major hybrid characteristics of mommyblogs. First, looking at examples of "unusual" motherhoods (e.g., mothers who are sex workers, transgendered mothers, or mothers with addictions) will illustrate how mommyblogs provide an astonishingly diverse array of representations of motherhood. The second hybrid analysis will consider individual mothers as hybrids by looking at the ways that bloggers narrate their motherhood identity beyond the realms of their mothering practice. By presenting three-dimensional and detailed versions of maternal subjects, mommyblogs (especially those written by women who come from non-normative social locations) can significantly shift static notions of mothers and maternity beyond the "tidy characterization" that *Her Bad Mother* blogger Catherine Connor notes is impossible. This diversity and richness implicate a new understanding of motherhood that rests in the interstices and inconsistencies rather than a coherent and consistent motherhood script. "Hybridity" thus emerges as a means of considering the many mothers who blog as well as the many "mothers" who emerge in any given blog written over time in the context of an evolving and complicated life.

Motherhood from the Margins: The Need for Diverse Motherhood Stories

Considering the ecological definition of hybridity – the melding or merging of disparate species – reveals both negative and positive ways that the concept has been used. Positively, the ability to hybridize has led to stronger corn, taller flowers, and disease-resistant animals. Yet the development of hybridization, scientifically speaking, led to concerns with miscegenation and racial purity; hybridization of humans was seen, by its detractors, as unnatural. An examination of traditional motherhood reveals the seeds of this resistance to hybridization. Following from the anti-hybridization stance has been a commitment to racially matched, heterosexual, and married families. In returning to science, however, there is evidence that the presence of tremendous diversity in fact strengthens ecological systems. Likewise, the emergence of a wide variety of different family combinations, demographic characteristics, and parenting practices in mommyblogs presents a very robust version of motherhood that begins to interrupt the ubiquity of "traditional" families recognized by patriarchal motherhood. Mothers with disabilities, queer mothers, mothers experiencing poverty, mothers from diverse ethnic, racial, and religious locations and myriad other "Other" mothers are writing in the mamasphere, exposing experiences that are not available in traditional motherhood stories found in magazines and books or on television. These stories do not merely teach about different mothers singly, but, as a collective, they change understandings of motherhood by shifting a societal perception of mothers that is deeply normative.

Mommyblogs increase access to non-normative maternal experience to an extraordinary extent, greatly outstripping the variety of maternal experience that has been documented offline. At the same time, it is important to remain critical of the limitations of, and constraints placed on, that diversity. Of course, most of the world's mothers do not exist online. Nonetheless, the mamasphere has opened the door to eavesdropping on literally millions of mothers' experiences that were simply not accessible before mommyblogs.

While I will endeavour to showcase the diversity of the mamasphere as a whole in order to establish hybridity and diversity as characteristic of mommyblogs, the nature of this project makes that undertaking intensely difficult. Specifically, I cannot provide samples from the millions of mommyblogs that exist, or even from all of the thousands that I have, over time, read. While I thus deliberately sought out a number of diverse blogs to establish the hybridity of the mamasphere, it must be taken for granted that whatever number of examples I provide represent only a tiny fraction of the full range of maternal experience documented in the mamasphere. Nonetheless, by looking at some examples of maternity not seen elsewhere, the range of possible mothers, families, and parenting practices can begin to be considered.

Transnationalism and Hybridity: *Gaza Mom*

Within transnational feminist literature, hybridity is an oft-used concept that interrogates the hyphens of individual identities (such as Arab-American) and often finds them wanting. Ella Shohat and Robert Stam (1994) usefully articulate this tension in *Unthinking Eurocentrism*, as Shohat (1998) does independently in *Talking Visions: Multicultural Feminism in a Transnational Age*. In considering the impact of subjects living constrained by hegemonic discourses, Shohat, Stam and others (including, notably, Kaplan, Alarcón, & Moallem, 1999) consider the simultaneity of resistance and submission in postcolonial subjects. Such a reading sees the hybrid as

> an important concept in post-colonial theory, referring to the integration (or, mingling) of cultural signs and practices from the colonizing and the colonized cultures ("integration" may be too orderly a word to represent the variety of stratagems, desperate or cunning or good-willed, by which people adapt themselves to the necessities and the opportunities of more or less oppressive or invasive cultural impositions, live into alien cultural patterns through their own structures of understanding, thus producing something familiar but new). The assimilation and adaptation of cultural practices, the cross-fertilization of cultures, can be seen as positive, enriching, and dynamic, as well as oppressive. (Lye, 1998, section 2, para. 10)

Hybridity, by this definition, serves a dual role. On the one hand, it acknowledges the tension inherent in undertaking a practice under oppressive conditions (e.g., mothering under patriarchy). On the other hand, it sees the circumstances that this tension creates as rich with possibility. Such a reading thus allows us to remain clear-sighted about the very real deficits of dominant discourses of motherhood and the ways that they limit both mothering and mommyblogging, while simultaneously considering the interesting opportunities presented by the tension between patriarchal motherhood and mothering work.

The mamasphere is full of examples of the specific adaptations that Lye references above. *Gaza Mom* blogger Laila presents one such adaptation on the part of her young son. This mother lives in exile from Palestine and though raising her family within a very normative gender structure, is extremely politicized with respect to her ethnic and national origin. The influence of this blogger's political orientation on her mothering is evident in this example, when her young son was asked to write his address down at his US school:

"Gosa?" I asked.

"It says Gaza," he said matter-of-factly.

"Oh – I see. But that's not your physical address, you live in Columbia, Maryland," I instructed him.

"Mama, you don't get it, that IS my address, it's my hometown, even if I live here, that is my real address!" he insisted.

"But it's not even in the United States," I replied.

"So what? It's my city!" he answered.

Ok, obviously this was a losing battle. Forget about explaining geography and the limits of physical boundaries to a 5 year old. What does it matter in his mind anyway? His "city" is Gaza; he is IN Gaza, even though he is physically present in the United States [2]

Laila uses her child's experience as a way of theorizing her own displacement and transnationality as a subject who is pulled between two different homes. Her son, free from the constraints of knowledge about physical space, can experience his hybridity in a complete way by acknowledging that he is simultaneously in two places. This moment is reminiscent of Karen Dubinsky's (2007) description of the "hybrid baby" as "those children produced by the movement for interracial adoption in post-World War II" (p. 142), subjects with both the burden and benefit of ambiguous social and geographical markers.

Both Laila of *Gaza Mom* and the hybrid baby exemplify the hybrid as "transnational sensibility," explicated by myself and Silvia Schultermandl in *Growing Up Transnational*:

A transnational sensibility begins by looking at life in and on borders, yet it goes beyond these inarguably contested subjects. It involves looking at the person who is looking and can be fruitfully applied to hybridized subjects as well as to those whose identities are presumed to be fixed. As such, this transnational sensibility sees a lack of fixity as simultaneously inevitable and rich in possibility. A transnational sensibility is both a methodology and a mode of inquiry: a way of seeing and deliberately *not-knowing*, a way of living within the spaces between questions and answers. (Friedman & Schultermandl, 2011, p. 5)

This transnational sensibility can be usefully applied to bloggers who are not necessarily explicitly politicized, but whose narratives are nonetheless evidence of "other" motherhood by virtue of their racial or ethnic identities.

The relative wealth of writing from nonwhite mothers online responds to the almost complete absence of representations of nonwhite motherhood in more traditional mothering texts. As Patricia Hill Collins (1987) documented with respect to black families in "The Meaning of Motherhood in Black Culture and Black Mother-Daughter Relationships," some of the issues facing black mothers were quite different from concerns about motherhood put forth by the women's movement or even present day feminist mothering texts. As Hill Collins argued, motherwork may be venerated within black communities and, to poorer families, economic contributions are viewed as a de facto contribution to mothering work, rendering the oft-described guilt of the working mother irrelevant. Yet not all mothers of colour are necessarily describing an existence that is different from mainstream accounts of motherhood. A less nuanced analysis would see depoliticized mommyblogs (especially those written by mothers of colour) as potentially regressive. A transnational sensibility, by contrast, engenders an understanding that the addition of both politicized and nonpolitical mothering narratives to the largely white canon of mother stories enriches perceptions of motherhood, albeit in potentially more subtle ways.

Mainstream Black Motherhood: *The Young Mommy Life*

Tara, author of *The Young Mommy Life*, seeks to explicitly disrupt traditional motherhood stories. She argues that she created her blog "in 2008 to address the serious lack of attention paid to 20something moms in mainstream media. You won't find $500 strollers here or advice on how to fire the nanny. It's a real look at motherhood through the eyes of a 23-year-old mommy of two. Sit back and enjoy."[3] This young mother, however, is still controlled by the same good mother myths that hold sway over "mainstream" mothers.

When Tara found herself unexpectedly pregnant at age twenty before completing college, her expectations for her future were derailed. The focus of Tara's writing is on her journey back towards the type of life that she had once hoped to achieve, one that includes professional success. Her blog reveals both her struggles in maintaining balance as well as her triumphs in achieving success. While she chronicles young motherhood, her own experiences are firmly entrenched in middle-class values and result in an account of her (married, double-income) life that deviates surprisingly little from more mainstream parenting accounts.

Tara is, herself, exceptionally critical of single mothers and unmarried young mothers, thus maintaining good mommy myths despite her purported foray into "difference." Her blog is largely about tips for saving money that assume a level of class privilege that allows enough money for some to be saved. While a young mother, she documents her experiences of parenting with a committed partner at the tail end of college and through graduation, quite a different life than that generally associated with "young moms." Tara, by presenting an alternative narrative of black young motherhood, does more to disrupt the stereotypical perception of this group of mothers than she does to provide an account of motherhood outside the centre. Tara chronicles her experiences in home buying and sharing care with her partner and balancing work and childcare. Her life is busy, complicated, overwhelming, and hard, but in ways that are more consistent with traditional motherhood than with many of the young black mothers she purports to represent.

A transnational sensibility allows us to see the importance of Tara's blog's inclusion in the canon of mothering narrative, but also the limitations to her particular narrative and her attempts to generalize her own experience. Tara's blog could be seen as a site of resistance by considering the essentialized version of young black motherhood as limited and stereotypical. Her self-congratulation and judgment, however, position her instead as someone who is getting motherhood "right" rather than as a blogger contributing to a more nuanced reading of a specific social location. Tara blogs at an additional site titled *Black and Married with Kids*. The title of this site is fascinating in that it acknowledges the racism and false assumptions made about black families as being "broken" in greater numbers than their white counterparts, yet maligns alternative family structures even as it attempts to respond to that essentialism. As a result, both of Tara's sites say more about who she isn't and who she wants to be – the perfect patriarchal "mommy"– than who she is.

The complications of Tara's identity categories were made especially apparent when she was targeted as the recipient of a Disneyworld vacation. Tara was selected because she was a black mommyblogger; black bloggers were specifically targeted to help launch Disney's introduction of the first black Disney Princess. Yet Tara was undoubtedly also selected because of her facility in fitting into mainstream notions of motherhood. One wonders whether this blogger would have been included by Disney were she a young *unmarried* black mother of two, or if her class position as a member of a two-income family is as relevant to the sponsorship as her race.

When Tara learned that she had won the trip, she wrote,

> I don't remember the first time I heard Disney was making a new movie featuring an African-American princess. I do remember squealing with delight, dancing around the room, saying, "Finally! A princess who looks like me!" . . . In this [Disney] flick, Tiana is a working girl in New Orleans, determined to fulfill her shared dream with her father to open her own restaurant. When Prince Naveen comes to town, chasing his love of jazz music and a carefree lifestyle, mayhem and mischief ensues.[4]

Tara perceives the inclusion of a new black Disney Princess as evidence of progressive change and does not reflect on her own social location and the targeting of black mommybloggers as a potential example of tokenism. As a young black mother who nonetheless presents a very normative experience of motherhood, Tara herself may likewise provide only token resistance to the mainstream without truly exposing dominant discourses of motherhood.

In positioning Tara and Princess Tiana as tokens, it is tempting to be universally critical of them. Yet to do so invokes more complicated questions. Would the mamasphere be better off, in some undefined way, without Tara's inclusion? In the case of Princess Tiana, would an upper-class black princess have been better or worse than the "sassy" poor girl that Disney has invented to placate black audiences? To suggest that Tara, by virtue of her social location, has a greater obligation to be critical of racism and patriarchy is itself a racist and oppressive mode of thinking: surely dark skin does not bring with it an obligation towards critical thought? In some respects, in fact, Tara's presence as a conservative young woman of colour is radical because it interrupts a discourse that links racialization to politicization. On the one hand, then, Tara's blog can be read as evidence that the presence of non-normative mommybloggers is simply cosmetic diversity, lacking substance. On the other hand, however, Tara can be seen as a unique individual who transcends the limited roles allowed her: she is not a poor, black, teen mom, and she is not a radical political black mother. Tara's blog thus serves as a reminder that black mothers are themselves much more diverse than the limited identities present in offline accounts would suggest. Despite herself, then, Tara shows some of the hybridity of the mamasphere even as she bolsters patriarchal motherhood in her writing.

Motherhood and Ethnicity: *Devis with Babies*

Devis with Babies is a site written by a mother of South Asian Indian descent (initially with another friend) seeking to chronicle maternal and cultural experiences of South Asian women. Deepa opens the blog by writing, in her first post,

> Even thus far into writing this blog, Monica and I vacillate on what exactly the bond is between Indian moms; is there something about us being Indian that makes our experience unique, and that makes us want to self-select into, for instance, a blog tailored to other Indian mothers. To be honest, I am not really sure. What I do know is that at this point the label of "Indian" and the label of "mom" are firmly mine and firmly entrenched into my identity, as much as "woman," "daughter," "wife," "sister" . . . as I find out in funny ways through the years, being of Indian origin affects many little and not so little aspects of daily life in subtle and not-so-subtle ways, no matter "how Indian" you may be.[5]

Deepa interrogates her intersectionality and her internal hybridity, but presents her experiences as her own, in stark contrast to Tara of *The Young Mommy Life*. By suggesting that her story is hers alone, Deepa complicates traditional motherhood tropes even as she simultaneously mothers in a fairly traditional way. Furthermore, Deepa asks readers to look at whether her subjectivity is, in fact, unique due to her ethnicity, or whether *every* mommyblogger is a product of culture, tacit or otherwise. Her tagline reads, "The random musings of a random mom who randomly happens to be Indian." Foucault (1976) suggests that such hybrid and independent narrative, in chorus with innumerable other sites of resistance, may provide the tools for substantive change through micro-movement. Perhaps anticipating the World Wide Web, he wrote,

> Just as the network of power relations ends by forming a dense web that passes through apparatuses and institutions, without being exactly localized in them, so too the swarm of points of resistance traverses social stratifications and individual unities. And it is doubtless the strategic codification of these points of resistance that makes a revolution possible. (p. 96)

Foucault considers the possibility of power akin to pointillism: the net effect of myriad points of dissent. Significantly, however, by suggesting that power relations work through apparatuses and institutions "without being exactly localized in them," he suggests that the fluidity of identity allows bloggers like Deepa and Tara to provide points of hybridity and resistance. Deepa interrogates her motherhood within both dominant Western discourses of motherhood and her own culturally specific lessons about good mothers. It is her interrogation, however, and not her identity, that is potentially empowering. While Deepa is not necessarily a radical mother, she provides an interesting example of a less hegemonic maternal voice. For example, Deepa presents her response to the 2008 US election:

> The day after Barack Obama was elected President of the United States of America, my husband's boss called him into his office.
> "I know it's been a few months since you've been working with us," his boss said, "but am I pronouncing your name correctly?"
> This is one of the many reasons we are elated – no, jubilant . . . no, ecstatic . . . actually, no word exists that describes how happy we are right now – about Barack Obama. He is the literal "other" that we've always been classified as, and as such, he makes people take a second look at us, rethink their attitudes about or treatment of us, and possibly even treat us with more respect. At the very least, he makes people think about how they're pronouncing our names.[6]

By highlighting many of the commonalities of motherhood as well as the unique distinctions that characterize all mothers – and not just those from non-normative social locations – the mamasphere problematizes and interrupts dominant discourses of motherhood; further, it extends our understanding and analysis of motherhood by including even mothers who are not explicitly radical as hybrid subjects.

If, as Foucault surmises, resistance must come from multiple sites simultaneously, then equally such resistance cannot be squarely placed on the shoulders of bloggers of colour, queer bloggers, or others who deviate from the mythical mainstream mom. To do so is to maintain the racelessness of white bloggers, and to expect non-normative bloggers to shoulder the burden for their ghettoization, which sets up an impossible task; decrying marginalization from the margins cannot garner the attention of the centre. Foucault's approach to power relations, then, allows us to consider not only the power of myriad voices, but also their complicated and contradictory positionality. On the one hand, Deepa's subjectivity as a brown woman allows her access to certain insights she might otherwise miss; on the other, Tara's marginal social location as a black woman allows her to reify the centre and aspire towards it ceaselessly. The writings of mothers even further on the margins likewise complicate the story of motherhood written from the inside out.

Mothering and Power: *The Dominatrix Next Door*

The blogger behind *The Dominatrix Next Door* first became a mother at fifteen years old and had three children in rapid succession. Now in her late thirties, the author of this blog chronicles her experiences with assisted reproductive technology in an attempt to get pregnant for a fourth time, many years after her initial foray into motherhood. These musings are skilfully blended alongside her discussion of her job as a professional dominatrix.

The dominatrix's narrative of motherhood is nontraditional in a number of ways. Her experiences as a sex worker are rarely represented in mainstream media, let alone alongside discussions of motherhood. She is also simultaneously a teen mom, grown up, and a mother parenting at a relatively older age. Her writing thus blends her experiences as a sex worker with her comparisons of mothering at different life stages.

She discusses a mothering rite of passage – a baby shower thrown for her by her friends – that was given a very special twist:

> Last night I went to my first real baby shower ever. Yes, this is my 4th baby, but I have never had a real baby shower. I had a mother-in-law shower, in which a bunch of people who my former mother-in-law knew came over when I was 15 and pregnant with my first, clucked-clucked at my tender age and talked amongst themselves. But never a real gathering of my friends to celebrate my rotund and expecting state. And strangely enough, while my vanilla friends have been rather distant and my kinky Domme friends have been warm and supportive, . . . they [the Domme friends] were the ones who through [sic] me the shower.
>
> So, it was not at all what one might call a normal baby shower. It was after all, held in the dungeon. And there were servants. Also? Tons of unbelievably cute baby gifts wrapped in the most adorable paper and ribbons. And, and of course, cupcakes with rubber ducks, baby bottles and little diapers on top of them! A typical baby shower. No?
>
> As we talked and laughed the slaves brought round after round of tasty snacks and refilled our drinks. Every once in a while one of the other Mistresses would tease, spank or humiliate the slaves and we would all giggle

loudly and talk amongst ou[r]selves about how much we enjoyed our chosen profession. Yup. A very typical baby shower.

It was an amazing bonding experience in a weird, weird way. In addition to the whole ridiculousness of the setting, there was quite a bit of reminiscing about their pregnancies, even a couple that ended in abortion; after all, we all have a right to choose. And may that NEVER change.

Right before the desserts started, it was decided that since we didn't have traditional games, that perhaps the two slaves should diaper each other and serve des[s]ert in nothing but, in one case, a bow tie and a diaper, and in the other, a leather vest, big leather boots, and a diaper. We even made one subbie bur[p] the other. Just what I always thought a baby shower would be like!

The whole experience made me realize what an amazing set of friends I have and what a strong bond I have with them. One I hope will never fade away even long after I retire. This is what I wish people who are against legalizing or even decriminalizing sex work could see and understand. These are amazing women who have chosen this lifestyle and made a business of it. They have never been harassed or forced into it. Please go after the pimps and the kidnappers and stop the human trafficking. But please, leave me and my friends to run our businesses, live our lives and enjoy our special bond.[7]

This blogger takes a very traditional pregnancy rite of passage, the baby shower, and shows how it may be politicized and transformed. The dominatrix references choice and abortion in discussing her very much wanted pregnancy. She also interrogates the traditional baby shower thrown for her as a young mother as unsupportive and oppressive. These observations resist popular notions of sex workers as downtrodden, as this author suggests that her experiences as a young mother were quite disempowering in contrast to her present occupation and social circle.

Power is present in this narrative in a number of interesting ways. The dominatrix is, perhaps unsurprisingly, very aware of the way that power enters her life, given that her profession is all about the exercise of power and control in very ritualized ways. She uses her power as a mommyblogger very deliberately and with care, and is able to control this medium in order to bring her particular mothering narrative to light. This mother is deeply protected by her anonymity and is able to tell a story that simply could not exist, except perhaps in an anonymous and retrospective memoir, without the power of Internet self-publishing. Her career in sex work calls on many discussions of gender and power: why this work is the most lucrative and rewarding option available, and how gender is troubled by this woman's role as a dominatrix coexisting with her use of sexuality as a source of income. Power, once again, is exposed as in aid of dominance, but in a complicated way. While this blog references power in both subtle and explicit ways, however, what is often most striking is the mundanity of the dominatrix's complaints and observations. She writes,

> Working as a Pregnant Dominatrix, watching my waist grow, and all my corsets start to look like relics from another era (heh, which some of them are) is hard! The stilettos are fine in the dungeon where the floors are flat, but throw in stairs, or any [obstacles], and I'm a goner.
>
> I think the main issue right now is my urge to work. Sometimes I'm really bummed to turn down what sound like fun (and financially rewarding) sessions from new clients who email, but lately, with the stress of the remodel and the ongoing eviction, I've just not been in the mood even to see my favorite regulars. I don't feel creative or inspired. I don't feel like I have that 'zing' that they have come to expect from sessions with me. I'm pre-occupied, bulbous, clumsy and gassy.[8]

The dominatrix skilfully documents the tension between work and family and the challenge she faces in balancing both successfully. She admits to fatigue and disinterest. By highlighting a very normative maternal experience through a completely non-normative lens as a sex worker, the dominatrix simultaneously entrenches traditional motherhood and disrupts it. And this, perhaps, is the chief strength of the mamasphere: it doesn't give mothers power; it doesn't take it away. Power may be experienced differently online than offline, but ultimately, mothers in the mamasphere are held to the same standards of good motherhood that govern their "real" lives.

The ability of the blogosphere to document with immediacy a richness and breadth of experience allows readers access to both the diversity and commonality of experiences, showing life writing to be both its own form of activism and a form of maintaining the status quo. In showing how much mothers have in common, non-normative blogs may concretize normative mothering practices; at the same time, they may reveal startling differences between mothers. Thus the writing of non-normative mothers is not, in itself, radical or repressive: it is simultaneously a hybrid of both.

Anonymity: *The Renegade Rebbetzin*

For many mommybloggers, like the dominatrix, it is possible to present the contradictions and tensions of maternal life because of the anonymity offered by the mamasphere. Anonymity comes with certain pitfalls, however. A rich blogging life must be concealed from friends and families. Anonymous bloggers may also be kept from the commercial success of others – many formerly anonymous bloggers now blog publicly, linking their online personas with their real names on public sites and elsewhere, in order to take advantage of the financial incentives available. For bloggers willing to make these sacrifices, anonymity allows for an authenticity that may increase the potential for ambiguity and disruption, as well as the potential for the individual mother's hybridity to shine through.

Perhaps as a result of her anonymity, the blogger behind *The Renegade Rebbetzin* presents a fascinating intersection of a normative life described in a completely deviant voice. "Rebbetzin" is the Yiddish term for a rabbi's wife. Within Orthodox Jewish communities, the rebbetzin is meant to be a leader and an example of righteous womanhood to those around her. She is a community authority and in order to protect both her own credibility and that of her husband, she often remains at arm's length from the rest of her community and congregation. She is also meant to visit sick parishioners, provide an example of appropriately modest clothing, and parent her children flawlessly. In short, a "good" rebbetzin must be a shining example of good motherhood.

In her blogging, the rebbetzin documents an extremely conservative and normative motherhood, disrupted only slightly by her non-Christian religious identity. She has six children, works only sparingly outside the home, and is almost exclusively responsible for household management tasks such as cooking, cleaning, and childcare. While the life this blogger lives might not show obvious signs of resistance to patriarchal motherhood, a different picture emerges on her blog. She uses the anonymity of her online writing to express her frustration with her community, her marriage, and the isolation of her role as community leader.

The rebbetzin documents the poverty the blogger's family experiences (in the process resisting the stereotype of Jewish families as inevitably class-privileged). She writes, "We're broke. We are so broke it's almost laughable. The finance-related stress in my house is intense beyond description."[9] Her anxiety converts to macabre glee at the aging of her community, which allows her husband to earn extra money:

Funerals, you see. *He keeps doing funerals.* And Baruch Hashem [Thank God] they have all been for elderly people who lived full lives and it just seems to have been "their time." And once again, they haven't been people I personally knew. So while I do feel *somewhat* sick and depraved, perhaps I don't have to feel *as* sick and depraved as I hopefully would in other cases, given that my primary reaction to this news, after saying "Oh, I'm sorry . . . was he/she sick?" is as follows: *Cha-ching.*[10]

By lifting the veil and providing a window onto a mothering experience that is often hidden from view, *The Renegade Rebbetzin* has gathered a community of fascinated readers. Many are themselves Orthodox Jews who are familiar with the community norms this blogger details. In the comments section, commenters commiserate with the rebbetzin's frustrations and sometimes disagree with her perceptions. A robust dialogue thus emerges that simply could not occur in the personalized context of "real" life, where interactions between the rebbetzin and other Orthodox Jews would be held to community mores. Commenters from other social locations might never meet an Orthodox rebbetzin and would certainly never encounter one so willing to divulge the unseemly details of her life. These readers expose the essence of deconstruction, where, by virtue of shedding or resisting specific identity markers, a new and multidimensional community can grow. In the realm of motherhood, this deconstruction is sorely lacking and is bolstered by the unique characteristics of the mommyblog.

Gender and Normativity: *Transgender Mom* and *Unwellness*

The blogger behind *Transgender Mom* is, in her own words, "a transgendered lesbian mom" who has a baby with her partner.[11] While she shares that she lives in a conservative state, she refers to her partner as her wife and their union as a marriage. She writes a great deal about politics and her own certainty regarding her transition from male to female, arguing, "To me a future where I didn't transition was a blank emptiness. There was no such future. So I had no reason to be afraid or to feel any loss because of it aside from normal worries like fitting in. It wasn't really 'transition or death.' It's more like 'transition or something unthinkable.'"[12] She struggles with the ambivalence she feels towards another friend who is less certain about gender transition:

> Before I went on hormones and met my current wife I went through a similar period. In my own case it was because I could not be emotionally involved with anyone who didn't see me as female . . . I have to say that after having my first child I understand it a lot better. I know that if I thought I had to choose between having another child or two and being true to myself it would be a difficult decision to make.[13]

Transgender Mom suggests here that while her commitment to transition was very strong, she would have a hard time following through if her transition would limit her possibilities of having children. In arguing that "if I thought I had to choose between having another child or two and being true to myself it would be a difficult decision to make," *Transgender Mom* exposes a conundrum – the tension between self-identity and maternal identity – that is resonant beyond an analysis of gender.

Transgender Mom clearly identifies as female and intends to mother her future child or children with her new partner, but leaves a number of components of her identity and parenting status ambiguous: for example, she does not provide details on whether she was mother or father to her first child – biologically or socially – or whether she will provide biological material (sperm) in the conception of her next child. By leaving these details deliberately out of her blog, this mother forces us to confront our need to order these concepts in a stable way and moves us towards a hybrid lens that allows for these "facts" to become irrelevant to the parenting story she chooses to share. *Transgender Mom* thus rests in the grey area of gender and motherhood. By choosing what to reveal and which details to consider unimportant, Transgender Mom draws on the rich history of life writing, allowing for an interruption of a standard narrative of motherhood and gender.

Unlike Transgender Mom, Briar of *Unwellness* clearly explains her family structure and the gender identities – past and present – of her family members. At age nineteen, prior to his transition from female to male, Briar's husband Wes bore and nursed a child and continues to be a mother to that child. Briar and Wes's younger son, however, sees Wes exclusively as "Daddy." Briar is herself a new mother, nursing an infant when she writes,

> I recognize that I was in a highly unique situation in that my husband breastfed a baby long, long ago. So long ago, really, that he does not recall

any pain or major discomfort from the ordeal. Either 19-year-old boobs are just meant for breastfeeding in a way 32-year-old boobs are not, or he just doesn't remember. Or he is freaking perfect and never had a bad latch for a single moment, the asshole.[14]

Briar's struggle with breastfeeding is both humorous and all-too-familiar to many mothers. Likewise, her tone in lambasting her clueless husband is echoed throughout the mamasphere. Unlike Transgender Mom, Briar doesn't choose to foreground trans politics or transgender identity in her mommyblogging. However, if, as Judith Butler (1993) asserts, "the criteria of intelligible sex operates to constitute a field of bodies" (p. 55), then the unintelligibility of Briar's husband's body and his duality as both mother and father (albeit in temporally interrupted ways) challenge the notion of motherhood as an exclusively female enterprise. Rather than providing a narrative from the margins by pinpointing her husband's transgendered identity, Briar reminds us of the irrelevance of gender by casually mothering with a father-who-was-once-mother. Instead of being a dramatic and unusual family, Briar shows us that the day to day mundanities of parenting transcend her theoretically remarkable family structure.

If Briar is politicized, it is not because she is married to a trans-man. Rather, she is frustrated with her experiences of working and mothering and saves her analysis for this topic:

> I have always been blatantly honest with you, blog people, even when my position is childish or selfish or silly. And so I am honest now:
>
> Staying home with my kid is boring.
>
> I have another post in me somewhere about how I think everyone who can possibly find work should be working, how infuriating I find the state of our country [the United States] and its lack of subsidized childcare for families, how very, very serious Wes and I are about wanting to move to Sweden, and about how truly, truly screwed up I believe some kids to be because their previously hardcore working moms have stayed home decades too long. That one is sure to offend, though. I shall have to work up to it.[15]

Briar suggests that the hybridity of the mamasphere is not merely important because different bodies are represented but because, perhaps more importantly, unique points of view flourish.

Contradictory and Convergent Motherhoods:
Fannfare and *Friday Playdate*

By disrupting the notion of mother as an overarching and totalizing subject position, the rich and incoherent narratives of mommybloggers portray mothers as much more than simply selfless caregivers. Such a portrayal is much more consistent with the lived lives of mothers, both online and offline, than dominant discourses of motherhood would suggest. As Amber Kinser (2008) argues, " . . . failing to face the messiness of feminist mothering, of confronting what Susan Maushart calls the 'mask of motherhood' . . . will surely result in self-betrayal" (p. 124). Mommyblogs aim to avoid that self-betrayal, to contribute to "a growing urge to narrate *other* motherhoods . . . together with a slow, but inevitable, process of redefinition of the ontology of motherhood(s)" (O'Reilly & Caporale Bizzini, 2009, p. 13).

Mommybloggers present convoluted subjects that live far beyond maternity. For example, Amy of *Fannfare* largely writes about the day-to-day minutiae of parenting her two children, chronicling new words that her toddler has mastered and bemoaning sleepless nights. Yet her life, it seems, is interrupted by struggles that are often excised from traditional mothering stories offline. Amy's struggles became apparent in June 2008 when her husband posted the following message on her blog:

> Hello everyone. This is Amy's husband Shaun. Amy asked me to post here so that anyone checking would know what's up with her. She is in a 28 day in-patient rehabilitation program for alcoholism. Basically she got to a point in her struggle that's like standing in the ocean getting hit by a wave and then as soon as you pick yourself back up, another wave hits. She needed to take a time out and get professional help.[16]

Amy's personal story is positioned within the tangle of discourses that contextualize motherhood; she is one example of motherhood as complex and variegated.

To some extent, the hybridity of Amy's life and the complicated lives reflected by most mommybloggers are products of the genre itself. This can occur for several reasons. As Amy shows, mommybloggers, like all mothers, have interests and identities that exist beyond motherhood. In addition, much of the work of childcare is fundamentally uninteresting – mommybloggers introduce other topics of interest partially to ensure that they have something to say. Furthermore, motherhood as an identity intersects with other social identities and even a "simple" mothering moment will thus approach these identities as topics of discussion. Beyond this simplistic rationale, however, the mechanics of how mommyblogs are formed allow a more convoluted maternal subject to emerge.

Print memoirs about motherhood (often described as "momoirs," see O'Reilly, 2009) have motherhood as their central premise and thus nonmaternal pursuits are generally sidelined, edited out of the essential story. Blogs, by contrast, are often written quickly and have no intended narrative flow. In this respect, mommyblogs most closely resemble offline diaries in their focus on hybridity and multidimensionality; yet within mommyblogs, these meanderings are honed in dialogue with comments and other bloggers (to be discussed in more detail in chapter 4). The lack of temporality of mommyblogs likewise contributes to the emergence of complicated maternal subjects: since mommyblogs have no fixed end point, their narrative does not need to preserve a traditional arc. Instead, mommyblogs meander, touching on infinitely more than simply motherhood along the way. The identity of the individual mommyblogger is thus circumscribed by the primary narrative of motherhood, yet also presented as an incoherent and fractured account. Even normative mothers thus emerge as more complex and hybrid characters through blogging: their interests and ideas are chronicled, pushing motherhood beyond the realm of caricature and into the realm of reality, albeit a reality that is highly mediated and complicated.

Jay Lemke (2008) suggests that our positions as subjects are born of fear and desire. The tension between these axes is clearly recognizable within most mommyblogs. While fear is presented in the tacit (or explicit) pressure of dominant discourses of motherhood, desire – whether for objects, opportunities or people – tends to factor into the picture any individual mother presents on her blog, resulting in a hybrid and multivariant identity. Thus blogs often evolve far beyond their set mandate. Blogger Susan documented her significant shift in identity on *Friday Playdate*. She writes,

> Once upon a time, not so very long ago, I taught literature in a fabulous liberal studies program near Seattle. I spent my days pondering the origins of the novel, the relationship between gender and genre, and the impact of colonialism on the post-modern narrative. I drank lots of terrific coffee and the occasional mid-afternoon martini.

Now I live in Oklahoma City with my husband and our two small sons (Henry, 9, and Charlie, 7); I pass the time contemplating which superhero is the strongest, what park has the most shade, and how many ways vegetarian chicken nuggets can be garnished. In my spare time, I shop for shoes, preferably pointy-toed flats that will make me look less like a mom and more like someone you might want to have drinks with.[17]

Susan's hybrid identity formation is fascinating on multiple levels. On the one hand, she documents her very wrenching shift from the public to the private sphere. On the other, by suggesting that mothers are not people one "might want to have drinks with," she is expressing her ambivalence towards the subject position she is currently embodying. This dichotomy is, itself, worthy of discussion, but the process of blogging lays yet another level of identity formation onto Susan: emotionally, blogging gives Susan a way of synthesizing her seemingly disparate lives of mind and body, public and private, then and now. Tangibly, blogging leads to more and more opportunities, culminating in a blog that is only nominally about motherhood but instead documents Susan's writing jobs elsewhere, specifically in the arena of fashion. Susan thus emerges as a much more complex subject than her brief introduction might convey; it is likewise notable that this introduction, listed in Susan's "About" page, is also the first post of her blog. She is thus simultaneously trapped by the duality of her earlier subject position and evolving within the pages of her ongoing prose. Her desire (in this case for a life in fashion), has led to the evolution of the blog and with it, a subjectivity that incorporates, but is not restricted to, motherhood.

Hybridity and Advocacy: *Dream Mom* and *Live from the Wang of America*

As the parent of a severely physically and neurologically disabled teenager, Sue of *Dream Mom*'s parenting practice has been intensive and confined to the realm of preservation, undertaken since her son's infancy and to be completed only upon his demise. This mother is undertaking all the tasks of patriarchal motherhood, albeit in an unusual context, and has seemingly subsumed her career, identity, and virtually all of her time to her son's ongoing care. Yet she, too, is a more complex subject than she might initially seem. Discussing her son's Individual

Education Plan (IEP), she considers the performances she undertook to be taken seriously within the school system:

> It was difficult for me in those early days, having to learn the whole IEP system and to negotiate for Dear Son. I would make sure on the day of the IEP, that I was impeccably groomed, my hair and nails were perfect and that I always wore a suit. This was the early nineties and that is what professional women did. I wore a suit to these IEP's not because I had to, but because I wanted to send a message that I expected the best for Dear Son and I would take nothing less. The other thing that made it easier for me, was not to view myself at Dear Son's mother, who was negotiating his education, but to view Dear Son as my "client." When I was at work and working with clients, I always wanted to give my best to them. And who should I advocate more for, than Dear Son? Once I viewed Dear Son as my "client" it was a lot easier for me to go into these meetings and negotiate his education since it took a little of the emotion out of the equation and made it easier for me to be firm with them on what I wanted. And they did take me seriously.[18]

Sue thus rests at the hybrid of mother and career professional in order to more effectively undertake motherhood. Far from undermining the stability of motherhood as a point of advocacy, however, her complex subjectivity instead provides yet another template of resistance. Even in the example referenced above, Sue is able to shape-shift her maternal identity but does so in order to be a good mother, to gain the best possible care for her son. This instance is an interesting example of the hybridity of identity; but it is also an example of the tension that lies between an exercise in empowerment and sacrificial motherhood. In speaking from the margins, *Dream Mom* presents a normative maternal experience but delivers possibilities for maternal activism.

Gidge of *Live from the Wang of America* is raising four children including twin sons with autism. She acknowledges the pain of parenting non-neurotypical children:

> But, when the forms came home – the permission slips for them to participate in the Special Olympics – it nearly broke us. Who WANTS that? Who WANTS their children in the damn Special Olympics? I don't. I suppose if I were a better person I'd suck it up and smile but if you want honesty – then no. I don't want them in it.[19]

Gidge chronicles the specific hybridity of mothering children with disabilities. On the one hand, she is required to mother in a hyper-intensive way to ensure that her children's needs are met – her sons do not *want* to go to swim classes and hockey, but are rather *required* to undertake hours of therapy per week. At the same time that she is an advocate for children with autism publicly and privately, Gidge is extremely conflicted about some of her personal choices. She undertakes genetic testing with her last pregnancy to see if the fetus is likely to carry a potentially autistic gene. This step serves as a catalyst for her ambivalence:

> What freaks me out, based on some of the things we've learned, is that they can see autism (sometimes or all the time I'm not sure) as a microscopic chromosome error. They don't know how it's caused . . . but they can see it.
>
> What then gives me pause is that if they can see it – then in the future they can make decisions to eliminate it. And you know what I mean.
>
> I'm very pro choice – but based on the papers I signed which allow them to keep my chromosomes and DNA on file at Columbia . . . I just felt the way the wind was blowing. Genetic Selection will become a reality. I just participated in the process. I did it for selfish reasons – because I wanted to hear that my baby girl was ok. And it will be invaluable in detecting disease and other problems so you can be prepared at birth.
>
> I'm not going to worry about a future I can't change, and I'm really glad for all the good it will do. I'm just sad that someone someday might make a choice that would deny them curly headed boys who give kisses and love the Teletubbies.
>
> Because sometimes you don't know that you would want something until you are faced with it. And then you know you'd rather have that, than nothing at all.[20]

In her ambivalence, Gidge is grappling with the tensions between what is good for her, what is good for her family and children and fundamentally, what is good for a society as a whole. In the act of writing she challenges those who read to similarly grapple with the ambivalent and contested spaces of motherhood, and in this grappling hybrid mothering emerges. This hybridity is especially obvious around tropes of the good mother.

Interrupting Good Motherhood: *Peter's Cross Station* and *Any Mommy Out There?*

Understanding the origins of hybridity is helpful in considering its applicability with respect to mothers who blog. In *Hybridity and Its Discontents: Politics, Science, Culture*, Avtar Brah and Annie E. Coombes (2000) discuss the long history of the term:

> Because of its current popularization through cultural criticism, "hybridity" is often misunderstood as a purely contemporary concern. The genealogy of the term is, of course, more accurately associated with the development of the natural sciences, and in particular, botany and zoology, where it referred to the outcome of a cross between two separate species of plant or animal. (p. 3)

Brah and Coombe's useful reminder of the scientific origins of hybridity shows the power of crossing one species – or perspective – with another. Similarly, the genus "Good Mother" has been blended with "Bad Mother" and "Sacrificial Mother" has merged with "Empowered Mother" to create a tougher and unconventional synthesis. To read mommyblogs this way, however, is to entrench these expectations of motherhood, when in fact these different "motherhoods" were never truly distinct. Some of these archetypes have been used to repress mothers, to constrain mothering practice by maintaining ideas of good and bad. Others, such as models of feminist and empowered mothering (Green, 2004, 2009; O'Reilly, 2004), have provided tremendous insights into the ways that mothers can resist patriarchal motherhood by raising consciousness and the perceptions of the mothering work mothers do. Yet a clear notion of hybridity allows us to truly see the ways that all such archetypes are always blended and variegated, never truly distinct.

Shannon, who identifies as a white, Christian, queer mommyblogger, writes in her blog *Peter's Cross Station* about her experiences with her partner Cole and the raising of their two adopted daughters who are black. The nuances of Shannon's blog posts cover thoughts about sexuality, race, open adoption, spirituality, and myriad other topics, all illustrated through the lens of her own life experiences. As a mother with a nontypical family formation and an unusual path to parenthood, Shannon does not easily fit into stereotypical perceptions of motherhood and she considers these stereotypes in terms of both judgments made upon her and judgments of mothers more generally. She considers some of the tropes of motherhood and the pervasiveness of mother blaming, considering the specific example of Nadya Suleman, the mother who bore octuplets in early 2009. Shannon writes,

> I have to say that all the poison cast towards Nadya Suleman reminds me uncomfortably of the same viciousness cast towards mothers who don't meet ever narrower, ever shifting culturally normative standards for all kinds of other reasons. Can't anyone else see that the judgement hurled at Suleman is just a stone's throw from the judgement hurled at any single mother, regardless of how she came by her children? Got pregnant the old-fashioned way? She's a slut. Used a sperm donor and hired a nanny? She's a selfish old maid. Needs some public assistance? She's a leech on the taxpayer. Self-supporting? She's a workaholic.
>
> And those judgements are yet another stone's throw from the ones that plague other mothers. Stay at home? You're a door mat, a bore and a bad example to your daughters. Work for money and use daycare? Why'd you bother to have kids if you didn't plan to raise them? Used fertility treatment? Obviously the good lord didn't want you to be a mother and you went against nature. Adopted? You stole a baby from its real mother to serve your own desires.[21]

Shannon can clearly see that her family does not resemble the pervasive image of motherhood held up in most media. Shannon uses her own fractured and hybridized subjectivity to consider the impossibilities of good motherhood beyond her own family. As a result, Shannon's blogging both destabilizes archaic notions of good and bad motherhood and responds to them in a dynamic way.

Stacey of *Any Mommy Out There?* comes from a slightly more typical family arrangement than Shannon. She is in a heterosexual marriage and has four children, three biological sons and one daughter adopted from Haiti. In her blog, Stacey provides a thoughtful analysis of the political implications of transnational and interracial adoption. Good motherhood is especially complicated in this non-normative context, where seemingly minor exchanges –such as discussions of hair styles – become potentially difficult. Stacey abandons the desire for good motherhood as a monumental quest and instead aims for a single moment of validation, as in the following example:

I don't know why I ask her, I hardly ever bring up this subject. I prefer to let her take the lead. "Do you think [your hair is] beautiful?" [I ask her].

"Yes," she answers, emphatic and enthusiastic. "I think my whole body is beautiful, I think my hands are beautiful and I have very brown skin," she holds up her arm to show me as if it is a discovery of hers, "and it is beautiful too."

"It sure is," I barely choke around my sudden tears. I am struck dumb. Again. Yet again, every day in some small way that is also huge, I am st[r]uck dumb by my children. It is not a script I have fed her or an answer she thinks I expect; it is not something we have discussed directly before this.

The moment sinks in like sunlight on my skin. It warms my core. We have to take these small triumphs, let them bask us in success, let them wash us in certainty. We have to take these moments for what they are and not question or second guess or wonder, just say to ourselves, briefly convinced it is truth, "I am an impatient and imperfect parent, I make mistakes, I stumble, I have no idea, for the most part, whether I am doing this well, but I am doing something right."[22]

In this example, Stacey is responsive to her daughter, but also willing to acknowledge her own hard work. She thus interrupts the idea of good motherhood as endlessly sacrificial by giving herself a timid pat on the back. Stacey's hesitation at presenting herself as a good mother is born of the some of the same ambivalence and insecurity that many mothers face. In Stacey's case, however, her own sense of herself as a good mother was called into question when she chose to adopt. While Stacey's family is now comprised of three biological sons and one adopted daughter, at one time Stacey also had an adopted Haitian son. After a very traumatic period, Stacey's five-year-old son left her family, a situation known as "adoption disruption." Stacey's sharing of this unique situation is a further example of the hybrid diversity of the mamasphere – there are few mentions of adoption disruption within mainstream parenting material, or even within mainstream adoptive material – but also of her complicated reckoning of notions of good and bad motherhood. Stacey narrates all the pain and ambivalence of this experience:

I read and read about attachment disorders and control issues in older adopted children. The best advice was in my head. Do not show anger, do not react, instead respond from love, keep him close. Yet our relationship spiraled downward. He acted out, I struggled to remain calm. My downfall was our babies. I simply could not control my reaction when he targeted them. My fears, of failing to protect them, failing to give them a safe and happy childhood, failing to create the large, happy family that I wanted to raise, triggered my own stress reaction and I lost control. I snapped at him and sent him to his room. He raged and beat the wall and drooled. Just when he most needed me to pull him closer, I would send him away from me, physically, because I needed the space to avoid yelling and screaming at him, but more damaging, emotionally, because I could not deal with my anger and fear. I failed him as a mother again and again.

Researching attachment therapies on-line brought a desperate word to my attention. A word I had never heard in all of my adoption research. Disruption – the technical term for the act of dissolving an adoption and placing an adopted child in a second adoptive family. Prior to attempting to parent our son, I might have harshly judged someone who adopted a child and then "gave them up" or maybe "gave up on them." Sitting at my computer, the word rang like a perfectly pitched note through my whole body. That was it. That was us. We were disrupted. Our lives were disrupted. Our children were disrupted. As an adjective and a verb, it perfectly described our family.

I still cry. There is so much guilt. I still lie awake at night and relive those months. What could I have done differently? With more patience, could I have broken through and begun bonding? I still wish he was ours, but happily so. Selfishly, but honestly, a lot of the pain involves my self-image. I still wonder if I am a terrible mother. The answer hurts because it is not simple. The answer is no. And yes. I am a wonderful, dedicated and determined, well-read, usually-patient, often-hurried, sometimes quick-tempered, incredibly loving mother to our three babies. I was a terrible mother for him.[23]

Stacey allows herself to live within – and reveal publicly – the tension between being simultaneously a good and "terrible" mother. Stacey explicitly premises this post by making clear that she is taking the risk of writing precisely because she has heard from another mother who is struggling with disruption and is feeling deeply depressed. Yet to other mothers who do not necessarily come from this experience, Stacey also turns a valuable lens onto a facet of maternal experience that is simply absent from most other public accounts of motherhood, be they media, theory, or life writing. In interrogating her own experiences, including her own potential "harsh judgment" of someone who would make this choice prior to her own experiences, Stacey disrupts our understanding of motherhood as both ceaseless and self-sacrificial – she is simultaneously a mother who gives her all and a mother who gave up. Yet she gives these revelations in a voice that is neither defensive nor completely at peace. She confides her guilt and ambivalence but also boldly makes a case for why giving up her adopted son was the only way forward for her family. In so doing she explicitly conceives of herself as both a good and bad mother, living within that tension and contradiction.

Writing from the Centre: Star Bloggers and Hybridity

To return to Foucault's points of resistance involves a move beyond a traditional focus on identity politics. At the same time, however, we must be cautious in our realization that many "star" mommybloggers – the mommybloggers who are, ultimately, drawing a huge level of readership – seek to undermine the constraints of dominant maternal discourses from the safe confines of largely normative social locations. According to Joan Scott (1992), "The project of making experience visible precludes analysis of the workings of this system and of its historicity; instead it reproduces its terms" (p. 25).

Such a reproduction may perhaps be seen in looking at popularity in the mamasphere. A close look at four very popular blogs initially gives the impression that only mothers from mainstream social positions can gain popularity. Yet a closer look at these blogs – Heather Armstrong's *Dooce*; Catherine Connors's *Her Bad Mother*; Alice Bradley's *Finslippy*; and Eden Marriott Kennedy's *Fussy*[24] – allows for a different reading.

All four of these very popular mommybloggers have common demographic characteristics: all are white, married, class-privileged, and physically able (though all, interestingly, suffer from fairly serious mental health challenges). Yet each also rest as hybrid subjects – they have each evolved throughout their abundant archives, have shifted stances on mothering topics and have documented an incredible range of issues and concerns relevant to mothers – abortion, same-sex marriage, disability rights, and ongoing coverage of multiple elections, to name a few. Thus, they emerge as so much more than the sum of their demographic parts. They are unique and evolving individuals presenting a collective and developing motherline. While it is thus important to note that there is a fairly clear glass ceiling within the mamasphere that limits the ability for bloggers from non-normative social locations to achieve the extreme popularity and concomitant monetary success that the stars discussed here have found, popular mommybloggers nonetheless provide a more variegated and hybrid picture than their demographic characteristics might suggest. Furthermore, the one key characteristic that unites these mommybloggers is a particular (and arguably peculiar) form of maternal activism that draws upon their high readership.

It is important to note the extent to which "star" bloggers are among the most vocal critics of patriarchal motherhood. Eden of *Fussy* writes in the byline of her blog, "We're not happy until you're not happy." Beginning in her son's infancy, Eden used her blog as a lifeline during the worst of her maternal frustration. Heather of *Dooce* chronicled her experience of postpartum depression but now, in parenting her second infant and restored to more robust mental health, is still completely irreverent about motherhood. Until recently, in her "About" page, Heather wrote, "I am a Stay at Home Mom (SAHM) or a Shit Ass Ho Motherfucker. I do both equally well."[25] While Heather's mocking of motherhood has garnered her a fair bit of criticism, it is notable that it has similarly drawn her a high level of acclaim. Indeed, across the mamasphere, mothers who decry motherhood and call out the systemic inequalities inherent in parenting are met with cries of recognition, creating a hybrid view of motherhood that displaces traditional views of supplicant and self-sacrificing mothers.

Each of these popular bloggers has been persistently ruthless in unmasking patriarchal motherhood and most have used their influence to decry perceived moments of social exclusion. For example, Catherine of *Her Bad Mother* called attention to discriminatory airline policies when she was told she had to cover up while breastfeeding on a flight; her outrage led to hundreds of letters written and an eventual apology from the airline. Likewise, Heather used her million-strong Twitter following to attempt to locate a mentally ill individual who had gone missing. These bloggers thus display the possibilities of seeing "just a mother" as an increasingly powerful subject position that lives simultaneously in public and private spheres and draws on social relations rather than more traditional sites of networking.

While it is tempting to see the funny and irreverent prose of these popular bloggers as simply a cosmetic response to patriarchal motherhood, there is an interesting moment of disruption in their status as stars. Specifically, there is a clear correlation between the unmasking of motherhood and popularity: readers clearly want to see motherhood's central myths contested. Equally normative bloggers who are ceaselessly celebratory about motherhood simply do not garner the same attention. It is obvious that the unmasking of motherhood, rather than simply normative social location, is directly related to popularity within the mamasphere. More importantly, each of the star bloggers draws on her own contradictions to amplify her voice: each owns her own adherence to "good" motherhood as well as her fear of being "bad," and it is perhaps this honesty and openness to contradiction that makes their blogs so powerful and so readable. While these bloggers have achieved fame within their own rarefied circle, then, they have not done so at the expense of becoming experts – their prose stands in stark contrast to the expert texts that guide traditional motherhood, and as a result opens the door to a more nuanced and hybridized analysis of motherhood.

On the one hand, given the potent forces of racism, colonialism, homophobia, and classism that circumscribe mothers' lives, it is impossible to ignore the demographic similarities between star bloggers and the amplification of such normative maternal experiences, however contested. At the same time, however, it is important to appreciate the singularities of their experiences. Their lives, like those of all mommybloggers are internally inconsistent and document a range of experiences and ideas – about motherhood and otherwise. This range represents the hybrid motherhood that exists online, a hybridity that frames a very complicated and nonlinear site of interruption and disruption.

Why Does Hybridity Matter? What Does Hybridity Offer?

Mommyblogs are not ultimately organized into normative and non-normative designations: the majority of mommyblogs give such detailed accounts that individual differences become paramount and often subsume broader differences in identity. This individuality can be frustrating in its ability to minimize or silence structural analyses: since each individual position is endlessly explicated, common ground is as easily found as abandoned. Yet the mamasphere's response to difference is fundamentally poststructural: strange bedfellows are made as mothers from profoundly different circumstances find points of commonality; mothers who are often herded into identity silos offline may find as many points of dissension as commonality.

In this endless negotiation and dialogue, static notions of privilege and oppression lack resonance, and allies and opposites are no longer entirely salient. The implications of this approach to difference are potent: on the one hand, organizing around identity within the mamasphere is often extremely difficult and quickly founders. On the other hand, the ongoing dynamic dialogue is an undeniably compelling monument to the collective voice of many women writing from an unprecedented range of positions. In learning about mothers who are different from "us," we learn about motherhood itself and, ideally, push the limits of that narrowed state into a more malleable version of itself. In learning about mothers "like us," we may confront our differences beyond our cosmetic similarities. But this, too, forces a consideration of the extensive diversity of motherhood. The mamasphere has exploded into a contentious mess, constantly arranging and rearranging itself around different issues, different "stars," and different hot topics, but generating an explosive energy in its frenetic movement. The hallmark of the mamasphere is instability, yet there is potential to see that instability as providing moments of possibility that might not be as visible in maternal accounts offline. To understand mothers that instability must be embraced.

It is critically important to note that as all mommybloggers write differently, all readers read differently. This is somewhat obvious with respect to social location, but it must be considered with regard to the use of different kinds of technology as mediated by social locations. With English as one of my first languages, I am able to read quickly and follow multiple blogs; thus I am able to access a wide range of blogs very efficiently. In order to do so, however, I read my blogs through a blog reader (NetNewsWire), which does not show embedded videos, so I skip those particular posts. My experience of the mamasphere is mediated by my own social location and use of technology. Readers with slower Internet connections may avoid any blog that is predominantly composed of pictures since these take too long to load into a web browser; likewise, any person who restricts their Internet use to the library will miss any of the audio features of the web. On an even more mundane level, websites look different depending on the web browsers through which they are viewed: not only are readers making choices of what to read, then, they are being subjected to other choices that are sometimes beyond their control. To add to the analysis of difference, it is important to consider that readers are not all encountering the same web.

In this poststructural moment the mamasphere can only be considered as an artefact uneasily, given that all readers encounter it in limited and incomplete ways. Instead, it is useful to focus on the mamasphere as a relationship, a place where motherhood is contextualized and debated. Critically, the "point" of the mamasphere is not to arrive at a conclusion, not to find "the answer." The mamasphere is, instead, about never-ending questions and an ongoing discussion. The implications of this endless discussion are mediated by difference, but rest in the moment between individual differences – in the mamasphere's relationality. In considering that relationality, then, it is to the cyborg that I now turn.

4 On the Cyborg: Dialogism and Collective Stories

Is anybody out there? Yes. A blog is a really weird form of communication. It's not like a conversation, since there's not that same back and forth, instead it's like holding a party in your living room where only one person is allowed to talk at a time. First the writer takes a position, or tells a story, and they get that down – their whole part . . . and then the reader becomes the writer and vice versa, and the new writer posts their insight into the topic – also without interruption. It's a complex way to communicate, and when I read the comments (and I read every comment on the blog) I'm frequently surprised at what resonates – and what doesn't. In a whole great big post . . . I'll make one reference to chocolate cake and the entire[ty] of the comments will go that way . . . and I'll sit there stunned. Cake? You really want to talk about cake?

It's a queer risk really, sort of a writers' book camp. What will happen next? The blog knows, but I don't – and trying to figure out what direction the blog-sled will go in after I give it a push down a hill is like trying to figure out why most food-shunning two-year olds will eat frozen peas. Intriguing, but hopeless.

– Stephanie Pearl-McPhee, *Yarn Harlot*[1]

Mommyblogs – like other writing online – exist, by definition, at the intersection of human and machine; they are heavily mediated by technology yet nonetheless are authored by humans in relationships with one another. Their cyborg nature is heightened by the fact that they document such very corporeal, physical work: that of procreation and tending to small (and not so small) children. Even among bloggers who document life with older children, the physical body, and the long-lasting effects of motherhood on it, are discursively present. Furthermore, mommybloggers rely on technology to mediate not only their writing but also the relationships they create and maintain. What results is a collective maternal subject that is fundamentally cyborg: the collective creation of a multitude of mothers writing together, but knit together through technology. This cyborg mother exemplifies the mamasphere in its focus on ambiguity and contradiction through the lens of responsive storytelling and community-building; mommyblogs are, like cyborgs, "wary of holism, but needy for connection" (Haraway 1985, p. 151).

Donna Haraway's cyborg foregrounds what is evident in the mamasphere – the creation of a supple and multiple reality through the blending of interactive points of view. Mommybloggers thus create these accounts not simply in unrelated multiplicity, but in relationship to one another, constantly reacting to one another to braid together a multi-threaded narrative. This narrative heeds Shelley Park's (2010) observation that "There is something . . . qualitatively new about the ways in which communication technologies, such as the Internet, transform our human subjectivity" (p. 63).

The relationality of mommybloggers is only one of their cyborg characteristics. The cyborg is unlimited by traditional notions of time and space – even the temporal expectations of human gestation can be interrupted and re-established in a machine age. This is clearly evident in the mamasphere, where the lack of temporality contributes greatly to the emergence of a complicated maternal narrative. While this lack of temporality is not unique to blogs (consider, for example, the open-ended narrative structure of diaries), the combination of this approach to time, coupled with the endless self-referential linking possible within the context of the Internet, allows for an interruption of traditional linear reading and writing. Mommybloggers thus invoke the cyborg to play with time, hearkening back to new motherhood or highlighting particular narrative moments through the magical robotics of hyperlinks.

This rearrangement of time, space, and narrative leads to the emergence of a "collective mother" in the moment of collective autobiography undertaken in relation to technology. This relationality, taken up on a large scale through the millions of mothers who blog simultaneously, creates a moment of what Leujeune has termed "networked intimacy" (quoted in Serfaty, 2004, p. 61). This collective cyborg mother is distinct from dominant discourses of motherhood and thus presents possibilities for the disruption of traditional mother myths, potentially leading to a re-visioning of maternal experience. Furthermore, this networked intimacy responds to the isolation and loneliness that intensive motherhood can engender. Mothers rally together around their shared insights (and also in argument), and as a result, the reification of sacrificial motherhood is interrupted.

This chapter will consider the cyborg mother with respect to three defining characteristics: the relationality of the mamasphere as an innovative form of maternal chronicling (most readily evident through the use of comments); the effects of time-shifting through technology on maternal accounts; and, finally, the emergence of a new collective view of motherhood through the reading of myriad simultaneous accounts of maternity. These characteristics will position mommyblogs as examples of new and innovative forms of maternal life writing.

The Cyborg Mother

Writing in 1985, Haraway used the cyborg (a contraction of "cybernetic organism") as a means of establishing the need for theory, and especially feminist theory, to move beyond a mistrust of technology and towards a consideration of the possibilities inherent in a more wired world. While Haraway's version of the cyborg is often understood as the specific example of the cyborg as machine-human duality, her overarching thesis rejects duality and looks towards complicated interrelationships between people, machines, and concepts that allow for more supple and convoluted understandings of lived realities such as those seen in the mamasphere. Haraway (1985) argues that "my cyborg myth is about transgressed boundaries, potent fusions, and dangerous possibilities which progressive people might explore as one part of needed political work" (p. 154). In understanding the cyborg as a mechanism rather than a form of rescue for antiquated forms of knowledge or theory, Haraway suggests that feminist theory must evolve with the cyborg and see its possibilities.

Responding to the dominance of identity politics in mid-1980s feminist thought, Haraway suggests that the cyborg shows the pitfalls of such an approach, arguing that fixed identity roles attempt to trap complicated realities by minimizing areas of difference. Yet, at the same time, Haraway does not suggest that identity categories be rejected outright. Rather, she argues that

> ambivalence toward the disrupted unities mediated by high-tech culture requires not sorting consciousness into categories of "clear-sighted critique grounding a solid political epistemology" versus "manipulated false consciousness," but subtle understanding of emerging pleasures, experiences, and powers with serious potential for changing the rules of the game. (1985, p. 172)

In this understanding, Haraway displays a transformative politic that is necessary for a cogent understanding of mommyblogs. In resisting both the seduction of identity categories and the chaos of their total annihilation, Haraway suggests that the daily realities of identity are both fractured and incoherent – and that this incoherence is enhanced by technology – but also that in embracing the tension between identity and difference, new possibilities for change emerge. Bon, author of the blog *Crib Chronicles*, considers some of these tensions and possibilities in her "cyborg momifesto." She suggests,

> our lives are couplings between organism and machine. our internal worlds are not circumscribed by the mere physical, and our external worlds – even and perhaps especially our days spent hands-on with the children we cherish – are not an existence solely of or in the body. this world, wherein we write and speak and interface and connect, is always present or available on the internal screen of our minds. it is a room of one's own, even if our houses overflow with toys and dishes and no space that is ours alone.[2]

Bon considers the ways that the Internet could extend mothers' spaces and allow a form of privacy – a cyborg "room of one's own" – despite the demands of children on physical and mental space. This capacity for a matricentric space is a radical potential of the mamasphere.

The cyborg lives at the intersection between feminism and post-modernism and attempts to respond to the tensions each exemplify in a functional way. By presenting the cyborg as equally a construction and an organic creation, Haraway (1985) suggests a reading of identity that highlights agency as well as the limitations imposed by existing structures of dominance. In so doing, significantly, she moves away from both formal postmodern theory (if such a notion cannot be seen as inherently oxymoronic) and classic feminist theory. She argues,

> The acid tools of postmodernist theory and the constructive tools of ontological discourse about revolutionary subjects might be seen as ironic allies in dissolving Western selves in the interests of survival . . . In the fraying of identities and in the reflexive strategies for constructing them, the possibility opens up for weaving something other than a shroud for the day after the apocalypse that so prophetically ends salvation history. (p. 157)

Haraway was almost prescient in her imagining of the present-day wired universe that allows (some) subjects unprecedented mobility of social location coupled with the capacity for almost limitless affinity. Specifically, the techniques that Haraway suggests as emblematic of her cyborg are displayed amply within the mamasphere and contribute to the interruption of maternal paradigms. Yet despite the radical potential of these ideas, thus far, the notion of the maternal cyborg has only been taken up fleetingly within feminist maternal scholarship.

Foregrounding the maternal cyborg online, Jaimie Smith-Windsor (2004) writes of the cyborg mother as "a breached boundary." In narrating her experiences of parenting an extremely premature baby, Smith-Windsor considers her daughter as a cyborg, kept alive by extensive use of technology that usurps the author's parenting role:

> There is no easy way to distinguish between the child and the simulated techno-Mother. The machine and the baby become symbiotic. "Sameness" governs the relationship between the baby and the machine. Their sameness means that they're mutually dependent on each other in order for life to continue. Technology is capable of simulating vital signs, of supporting life, of becoming Mother. (2004, A Critical Questioning section, para. 12)

In displaying her understandable discomfort with her situation, however, Smith-Windsor may overlook some of its possibilities. She argues that her daughter's early infancy moves away from a dependence on the mother, yet fails to see that this shift may simply present a new understanding of motherhood. She writes, "The machine can't ask: What would the world look like without mothers?" (2004, A Critical Questioning section, para. 27), yet she doesn't consider that perhaps this question is itself problematic, suggesting that the essence of the social construct of "maternity" is cultivated in the interdependence of infant and mother. Perhaps a better question might be, "What would the world look like with a more nuanced and open-ended view of motherhood?"

While powerful, Smith-Windsor's experiences rely on an orthodox understanding of Haraway's cyborg as simply blending machine and organism. Although Smith-Windsor arrives at a conclusion that disrupts static notions of maternity, she misses some of the nuances of Haraway's metaphor, which relies on techniques of connection and negotiation of time and space. Shelley Park (2010) suggests a different approach, looking at the ways that technologies allow for a new mode of maternity that is less reliant on physical presence. She considers the ways that she now tends to her children through various communicative realms such as cell phones, email, instant messaging, and social networking, terming these "technologies of co-presence" (p. 62). Park argues that "sometimes . . . technology enables a co-presence that physical proximity does not" (p. 56).

Looking at the cyborg mother within mommyblogs takes up these themes and considers them in relation to maternal accounts taken singly, but also, more importantly, in relation to one another. Many of the attributes that Haraway ascribes to the cyborg are readily apparent in the mamasphere; in reading mommyblogs as examples of cyborg motherhood, her theory is a meaningful lens for analysis.

Relationality

Considering the ways that discourse is both constitutive of dominant themes of motherhood and, itself, modified by these themes makes an examination of motherhood discourses online highly challenging. Mothers write mommyblogs in the context of dominant discourses of motherhood, but also in constant conversation with one another and with commenters. As a result, the mamasphere can be viewed as a dynamic organism, bound by discourses of motherhood yet constantly emerging to both obey and resist these discourses in dialogue. As a collective, the mamasphere allows for social movement creation in that it "helps in building a collective identity among participants and potential participants of the movement" (Nip, 2004, p. 233).

A simplistic example is as follows: blogger Kathy of *Groovy Gams* is not, strictly speaking, a mommyblogger. Rather, she is a "grand-mommyblogger," keeping her blog as a record of her grandchildren. On one family trip she writes, "Saturday we went exploring (read Leia's account here [link to http://monkeys-jump.blogspot.ca/2009/05/day-trippin.html]) and had an awesome time just driving and taking in the scenery."[3] Kathy embeds a link to her daughter's account of the same activity, allowing the reader to click over to Leia's description of events. Who is the true *Gams*? Who tells the truth about Leia and her children? On the very basic level of a family outing, the impossibility of "truth" becomes apparent and a cyborg storytelling emerges that allows as much to seep from the margins and moments in between as from the narrative itself. Such an account hearkens back to Mikhail Bakhtin's notion of polyphony, which "identifies the co-presence of multiple, often contradictory discourses within the same text, without any possibility of these discourses being unified by a single subjectivity" (Serfaty, 2004,

p. 61). In the realm of motherhood, this polyphony disrupts the idea of mothers as the holders of their children's stories, allowing instead a collective narrative to emerge that foregrounds subjectivity over documentary reality.

A focus on relationality is consistent with Haraway's notion of the cyborg seeking to destabilize the monolithic status of the individual subject (discussed in greater detail in chapter 5). As N. Katherine Hayles (2006) argues in "Unfinished Work: Cyborg to Cognisphere,"

> the individual person – or for that matter, the individual cyborg – is no longer the appropriate unit of analysis, if indeed it ever was. At issue now (and in the past) are distributed cultural cognitions embodied both in people and their technologies. As Haraway reminds us, the smallest unit of analysis is the relation. (p. 160)

Hayles's analysis provides a valuable point of entry to the mamasphere by highlighting the complex relationships between mommybloggers as, in fact, more important than the individual narratives taken in isolation. This notion is essential as a foil to dominant discourses that pit mothers against one another by creating false binaries (stay-at-home mothers vs. working mothers; breastfeeding mothers vs. bottle-feeding mothers). While these specialized silos undoubtedly exist in the mamasphere, the overall argument is often nuanced and enhanced by the multiplicity of voices and the richness of dialogue; such a reading draws on ideas of life writing as "the playground for new relationships both within and without the text" (Kadar, 1992, p. 152). Furthermore, as communities are continuously created (and disbanded) online, mothers are constantly acknowledging those communities and thus shifting their own narratives in response. This response is sometimes a strategy to bolster popularity or enhance monetization techniques, but most often it emerges as the isolation of motherhood – especially non-normative motherhood – is interrupted by virtue of the relationality of mommybloggers.

Providing one example, blogger Julie of *A Little Pregnant* writes about her own position as one of the most well-known and longest-running mommybloggers among women who are writing about infertility:

> I don't even know how to talk about this without getting teary. Several months ago I met in person someone I'd known inside the computer for

quite some time, a woman who's been a loving presence in the infertili webjournopixelsphere for years. We hugged, and as I tried to make my squeeze communicate even a fraction of my affection and gratitude, she whispered, "You saved my life."

That's not something I take literally or even personally – every single blogger in our community has been a lifeline, no exaggeration, for others, just by writing, listening, *being* – so I understood it to be a collective truth. But it's also not something I take lightly, because, my God, I mean, *you* all saved *me*.[4]

Julie chronicles the symbiosis between her own experiences being held up by her peers online when she felt most vulnerable, coupled with the ongoing power of her archive to continue to support and maintain others, even others with whom she does not explicitly have a relationship. While it is tempting to dismiss Julie's words as hyperbolic, the sentiment that she describes reverberates across the mamasphere as women discuss the ways that the ability to reach out, write, and read about their frustrations, triumphs, and the mundanities of motherhood have been truly life saving. The cyborg relationality of the mamasphere, then, can be seen not only as *constitutive* of something – a collective autobiography to be discussed in greater detail below – but also as *representative* of a process of community building and sharing. Viviane Serfaty (2004) suggests that this is the most notable characteristic of online life writing:

This is precisely where Internet diaries and weblogs innovate most radically . . . Not only do they make intimate writings potentially accessible to a multitude of readers, but they also make it possible to include the responses of the readers. In so doing, they set up a dense network of echoes and correspondences between diarist and audience and, more importantly still, they give it visibility. (p. 52)

Certainly, the capacity to simultaneously reach out to so many mothers in so many different places – geographically and sociologically – is unprecedented. As Stacey of *Any Mommy Out There?* writes,

I have been startled and tickled by how blogging connects me to other women – and a few men – across the country and the world. I am addicted to reading stories and finding writers that I enjoy. I love chatting with no restrictions based on time or distance. It's like the plot of a science fiction novel and a morning chat over coffee all wrapped up in a nice package and I don't even have to take off my pajamas.[5]

As in life offline, the relationality of the mamasphere is not without its negative characteristics. The power of negative interactions to limit authorial power and to uphold dominant discourses of motherhood shows that these dominant maternal expectations are not extinguished online. In addition, for the many mommybloggers who write in relative obscurity, the quest for connection and comments may likewise shift the maternal discourse away from authenticity towards a narrative that upholds the normative expectations of both motherhood and blogging. In order to understand the full impact of the cyborg mother and the relationality of mommyblogging on dominant discourses of mother-hood, then, the phenomenon must be examined in greater detail. In the following sections I will discuss the positive aspects of relational-ity; the negative aspects of relationality; what happens when relation-ality is not achieved; and, finally, the impact relationality has on star mommybloggers.

Positive Aspects of Relationality

In creating a collective account of lives lived, the stories that emerge in mommyblogs are, if not random, then perhaps organic products of dia-logue between mothers rather than singular monologues. Yet these dia-logues are unlike offline interactions in that participation can occur at distinct times and sometimes without the knowledge of the person who began the interaction. For example, when the blogger behind *Blue Milk* is dismayed about her two-year-old daughter's swearing (overheard at home), she writes about her feelings of concern and obligation,

> As it turns out I wasn't sickened. I had the decency to feel a little taken aback and so did her father who looked at me, eyes widened in surprise with a "so what do we do now" expression . . . I thought blankly for a sec-ond and then I remembered reading this post [link to http://www.lesbi-andad.net/2007/11/the-f-word-bites-baba-in-the-ss/]. Thank you blogging, you've taught me all I need to know about parenting.[6]

By clicking on "this post," can a reader access the "solution" that Blue Milk references, creating a response to this dilemma that is co-created by Blue Milk, the blog she herself reads, and the commenters who read her blog. The artefact that remains in her blog becomes a cyborg melding of many different opinions put forth in different platforms and drawing on both human and technologic interfaces. This melding results in the creation of new and continuously challenged mothering norms and serves as an essential foil to expert parenting discourse. In an increasingly child-centred era, this potential to participate in the creation of mothering norms is deeply radical. It draws on the grassroots of communal, dialogic mothering to knit together flexible and interruptible rules for how societies may function and how mothers may act. Blue Milk thus experiences her child's swearing while held within a network of support, rather than under the gimlet eye of a critical society.

If the cyborg foregrounds relationships as integral building blocks of society, the mamasphere likewise presents a capacity for relationship that has bolstered countless mothers throughout their parenting journey. Mommybloggers have come to rely on one another's words for support and validation. Catherine Connors of *Her Bad Mother* articulates this point strongly on *BlogRhet*, a collective blog designed for the discussion of blogging practice:

> Blogging mothers have done two things: they've created a network for themselves and they've given the rest of us front row seats into a performance that would have otherwise been completely missed. We get the jokes that would have sailed over the heads of their children, the expressions of serious frustrations that preoccupied husbands dismiss as petty, and the profound insights that would have been forgotten by the time they finally got a coffee break with friends, unable to remember what they were so eager to say now that they are forced to socialize distracted by the peripheral parenting that characterizes almost every activity at a particular stage of life.
>
> It might just be that historians and sociologists will eventually conclude that the blogging mothers have created a new kind of motherhood. Meanwhile, the rest of us are beneficiaries of their willingness – perhaps even their eagerness – to perform, at last, before an audience that can't help but applaud.[7]

Catherine's comments present a powerful validation of blogging practice as evidence of both community building and disruption of traditional motherhood – by providing mothers with a new way to interact, by documenting the minutiae of daily parenting on an ongoing and archived basis, and by viewing such minutiae as worthy of documentation. Blue Milk expands on this point, considering the ways that reading mommyblogs has enriched her mothering practice and lessened her isolation:

> I remember the relief I experienced when I first started finding and reading (and later writing) motherhood blogs on-line. That sense of it being ok, that someone else was going through the same thing, that I wasn't alone in what I was experiencing. I want mothers to be able to talk freely and honestly about their lives even when I don't share their outlook or agree with what they're saying (after all I don't have to read it if I don't like it). It's a powerful, therapeutic experience to find your voice.[8]

Blue Milk suggests a point that many other mommybloggers make: in presenting motherhood as a fundamentally individual task, the dominant discourse of motherhood breeds isolation among mothers. The mamasphere disrupts this isolation as mothers see one another's experiences through first-person life writing in real time. At that point in cybertime, connections are made.

Bobita, a feminist academic and mommyblogger, expands on this point in documenting her initial foray into the mamasphere:

> I spent 10 hours on the Internet that night. I read many, many blogs and instantly felt as if I had planted magic beans . . . and a magnificent queendom had appeared! In this queendom were mothers. Mothers struggling with the very same issues that I faced daily. Women searching for meaning. Women finding meaning in the singular moments of motherhood. Women slamming up against questions and uncertainty in the alternate moments of motherhood! It was one of the most validating experiences of my life. I felt understood and included in a profound way . . .
>
> And so I blog. It is my hobby. But ever so much more importantly, on most days . . . it is my lifeline.[9]

Bobita's writing speaks to the exceptional speed with which the mamasphere may connect to any given woman, as well as the capacity for this technology to create a dynamic archive of writings that may reach out, as a lifeline, to mothers in their isolation and frustration. As a counter narrative to the traditional mother, then, the cyborg mother emerges in the mamasphere as a potential source of empowerment and resistance across boundaries of time and space.

Fundamentally, the cyborg relationality of the mamasphere presents a complicated response to the individuated maternal subject. By exposing the daily moments of their lives, mothers empower themselves and give voice to their mundanity and their multiplicity, and they connect to an audience of peers who are likewise empowered and validated. The commonalities of motherhood and the very stark differences between mothers are thus wed in a deeply cyborg moment that exists, as India Knight (2009) describes it, in the "seismic – and I don't use the word lightly – difference the online world has made to women's lives, by holding a mirror up to them and celebrating the minutiae of their existence as if it mattered" (para. 1). This blend of attention to difference and focus on commonality exposes a powerful response to traditional motherhood discourses as well as tensions within postmodern feminism.

The mamasphere lives at the intersection of mother and other, of conversation and memoir, of audience and author. In threatening these "stable" spaces, the mommyblog is truly cyborg, a strange melding of seemingly disparate conceptual zones. In this dialogism, the self is both co-created and amended by the self in relation to others; a collective story emerges with discursive implications for each of its creators, and its readers beyond. While the brave new communication that emerges in blog writing might well be "weird," as Stephanie of *Yarn Harlot* concludes in the quote that opens this chapter, its weirdness allows for a compelling and responsive conversation to emerge that is distinct from the authority of sole-authored texts.

One of the key functions of the cyborg mamasphere is the capacity for non-normative mothers to find connections and to shed light on aspects of identity or parenting practice that are generally ignored within dominant discourses of motherhood, as seen in the discussion of hybridity. One example can be seen in the blog *Finnian's Journey*, written by Lisa. Lisa is a mother of six kids, one of whom has Down syndrome. While Lisa skilfully documents her initial sorrow and fear at learning of her son's diagnosis, her blog also articulates with emphasis here that blogging creates connections around shared identities:

When I first started this blog not quite 16 months ago, its only intended function was to create a central place to update friends and loved ones on how Finn was doing after he was born. Over time, through this blog, I became a part of a large, loving community of other families touched by

Down syndrome. The support has been invaluable to me. And from there, it has evolved into a means of raising awareness about Down syndrome, by sharing with the world (or at least whomever stumbles across my humble blog) a window into a pretty regular family's life with a child who has Down syndrome.[10]

For many other mothers whose parenting practice deviates from the mythical norm (whether those mothers be feminist mothers or military mothers, home-schooling mothers or academic mothers, or any number of other mothers whose parenting ideologies or social locations are somehow "deviant"), mommyblogs have the capacity to create a shared narrative and a community that acknowledges their unique space and, as argued in the previous chapter, resists the narrowing of identity to a single "unusual" narrative. Furthermore, connections are made beyond traditional identity silos wherein, through the relational interaction of the mamasphere, mothers may connect with others with whom they might otherwise have nothing in common.

Mommybloggers may also find that their connection with the Internet comes to represent a relationship in its own right. Some write of feeling frustrated when other bloggers neglect their responsibilities by posting infrequently; others write about their feelings of responsibility to their online community in posting frequently. Participating in communities is sometimes trying and difficult; similarly, the online relationality of the mamasphere presents not only positive but also challenging characteristics.

Negative Aspects of Relationality

To organize the relationality of mommyblogs into negative and positive traits belies the complexity of the interrelationships among millions of mothers online. This disclaimer notwithstanding, it is nonetheless important to understand the ways that the responsiveness and immediate audience reaction to many mommyblogs has, in some cases, maintained dominant discourses of motherhood and limited authenticity rather than allowing powerful truths to be exposed. Any given blog thus encapsulates the tensions between the desire for attention and adulation and the desire for authentic discourse and validation.

The cyborg mother is mediated by the relationality of the blogosphere and the ways that writing in such a responsive medium presents a potentially burdensome self-consciousness. Courtney of *CJane*

Enjoy It articulates this point skilfully when she argues, "If blogging is the new virtual community then comments are the currency. The more you have the richer and happier you are (so you think). It can cause complications with your confidence and plague you with self-doubt."[11] Courtney's comments suggest that while the cyborg nature of the mamasphere has created the capacity for immense connection and disruption, it has likewise created an environment that may foster insecurity and an overemphasis on popularity as currency. This concern with popularity may result in less authentic writing as mothers strive to toe the line with one another rather than truly considering difficult topics. It is also possible that some of the fissures opened within traditional understandings of motherhood – the boldest and most radical topics – may simply be too difficult to acknowledge and are thus quickly papered over or otherwise abandoned.

On a facile level, negative comments can cause authors to feel distressed. Since the content of most mommyblogs is personal, rather than simply editorial, negative comments may often be very personally experienced. Lucy of *Lucy the Valiant* is a mother who struggles with different methods of getting her baby to sleep. She writes,

> What is really distressing to me is how ANGRY people get on this topic. I am young. I am sleep-deprived. I am prone to late-night Googling. I really just want to have the facts laid out for me, without having to stumble across the "You are a cruel, horrible person who only cares about their own sleep and are teaching your child that you NEVER LOVED THEM, hope sleeping now is worth all the therapy you will have to pay for in the future, for a grown child who never speaks to you because, hello, you are a JERK!" comments, rebutted (?) with the "Shut up, maybe YOU don't show YOUR baby that you love them during the day, but MINE KNOWS that I love him, so I can sleep aLL NIGHT LONG, BIATCH." comments.[12]

On the one hand, simply receiving negative comments tends to provoke a response and an inevitable dialogue, with other commenters defending the blogger or commenter and sides being taken from there on in. These comments, while personally authored, tend to gravitate (as in the example above) towards the poles of "hot" Western mothering debates: breast versus bottle; attachment parenting versus other parenting styles; home schooling versus public versus private schools; home versus hospital births. It does not escape scrutiny that these debates are largely of interest to class-privileged parents. As Veronica Arreola (2008) wrote in *Bitch* magazine:

> When Mommy Blogger A waxes rhapsodic over the $5-a-pound local, organic heirloom tomatoes she picked up at Whole Foods, does that resonate with readers (or other mommy bloggers) who struggle to put an entire dinner on the table for $5? If Mommy Blogger B brilliantly paints the picture of how she had to fire her nanny over religious differences, can a working-class mom of color feel that story after her own 10-hour workday? This cross-cultural division extends to the comments section of blogs: What does it say to writers in a community when someone's snarky post about nanny stealing gets a ton of responses and another's post about explaining sexism and racism in the presidential race to her 10-year-old daughter gets not a peep? (para. 4)

Arreola's analysis is valid, yet ignores the extent to which the mamasphere succeeds in exposing non-normative parenting practices and social locations and in creating connections – based both on difference and moments of congruency between mothers – that bolster community. Nonetheless, the mamasphere, like the cyborg, is not immune to the broader social mores that underpin mothering, including a greater attention paid to the challenges of class-privileged parents. Ironically, the same mechanism that allows for a presentation of possibly the broadest spectrum of choices in existence, then, may curtail that power through the process of audience-community interaction.

Even in this reading, power is not singular or un-nuanced: negative comments may generate angry posts, and angry posts will generate controversy and often increase a blogger's popularity. Insofar as popularity or readership is a measure of power, then, controversy is immensely powerful. *Her Bad Mother*'s Catherine exposes this tension when she reveals a painful self-consciousness in blogging about her nephew who is dying of muscular dystrophy. Catherine presents the difficult tension she faces in wanting to expose her nephew's difficult journey publicly while also acknowledging that dramatic prose inevitably results in more readers visiting her blog: "I worry because I feel a little sick whenever I notice that Tanner is good for traffic. I feel sick even writing the words, *Tanner is good for traffic.*"[13] Significantly, Catherine reaches no conclusion apart from exposing her characteristic self-reflection.

Shana's blog, *Gorillabuns*, saw an immense surge in popularity following her son's tragic death to SIDS; her response to a few comments suggesting that she was to blame for her loss further bolstered responses to the site. The power of popularity, however, is neither linear nor straightforward, as Shana points out:

> When the shit hit the fan, so to speak with people commenting truly crappy and careless things, I started to re-evaluate what I am doing here . . . I guess after four years (as of this month) of writing pure mundane drivel, I've been found out. I worry how my blog is going to affect me or my children at their school. I worry that something that gave me such comfort after my Grandmother died with two children under two and a husband that traveled so much for many years has run its course for me. Mainly, because of the pressure in the back of my tiny pee-brain head does not want to not say something that is going to offend anyone and everyone.[14]

Months later, Shana is still cautious when she posts:

> I am very reluctant in writing this post as I will probably gather all sorts of crazy, stupid-ass comments as I am [wont] to do but I am going to spout forth this shit anyway. Just because but beware, I will go ape-shit on your ass if you accuse me of being an alcoholic, negligent person or worse, a totally shitty mother who doesn't deserve happiness in this world.[15]

What is notable in Shana's narrative is that, her disclaimer notwithstanding, she chooses to continue to speak her truth; she exposes the underdiscussed pain of losing a child, fiercely defends her characteristic irreverence and parenting choices and chooses to do so in the context of a potentially hostile, yet responsive, community. Her concerns regarding audience reaction undoubtedly shift her narrative, but this shift simply confirms the fundamental interactivity of the mamasphere as a dialogic medium. Shana does not write in isolation, but in relationship with her readers, presenting an account that may be different from her private musings, but that may nonetheless present a significant interruption of traditional mothering tropes.

Occasionally, the relationality of the mamasphere may completely inhibit mommybloggers, as in this example from Stacey of *Any Mommy Out There?*:

Want to know a secret? There is a very popular blog that I will not go
back to because I left this asinine comment that made me sound like I was
twelve. It wasn't mean or even rude, it was just dumb . . . I'd like to follow her on twitter because most twitterers do and I read a lot of one-sided
conversations [by] not following her, but I won't. I don't want to give her
a reason to remember my existence.[16]

Stacey's experiences are not unprecedented and show the extent to
which the mamasphere is an organic entity rather than simply a well-
designed tool for contesting dominant discourses of motherhood.
Again, then, what is of real interest in looking at the cyborg, relational
mamasphere is the extent to which relationality does not often yield
responses such as Stacey's. On balance, mothers successfully relate to
one another and use their interactivity to interrogate and negotiate the
difficult work of mothering within a hostile world. If, as Linda Warley
(2005) asserts, "the interactivity of personal home pages provides perhaps our best example of the 'self-in-relation' posited by some theorists
of autobiography" (p. 32), then what is the effect when this interactivity is not achieved?

The Quest for Relationality: Avoiding the Solitary Mamasphere

Highly popular bloggers arguably face the most scrutiny and negativity, something that will be explored in more detail below. Yet women
who are generally unknown experience the vulnerability of commenting practice differently. Shana's experiences notwithstanding, unknown bloggers without a major following might not have others to
rally in their favour when negative comments are made. Furthermore,
reading controversies in more popular mommyblogs may discourage
bloggers from entering into the fray and posting their ideas on potentially dissentious topics, even when such topics are those about which
they may require the most support and feedback. Yet for some mommybloggers, whether from diverse or mainstream social locations, the
trouble with comments is much more trite: people may not comment
at all, turning what may be, at its best, an interactive forum, into a virtual message in a bottle. Who is the author in the absence of a reader?
Perhaps of more interest, what is the effect of the deep desire for a relational narrative on mommyblogging practice?

Elisa of *Diary of an Unlikely Housewife* succinctly frames the tension
between wanting and fearing comments: "Sharing things online means

you have to be willing to get input you may not want, or like. And we are all comment wh*res, we all love getting replies to our tweets and comments to our posts, because that's what interaction is, right?"[17] Elisa goes on to articulate her challenge in receiving unsolicited parenting advice: does she speak her mind or maintain the peace? Of course, by blogging about this dilemma, she is already beginning to disrupt expectations of herself as a good and obedient mother; nonetheless, her comments are a reminder that the relationality of the mamasphere creates a quest for community that, in itself, shifts blogging practice.

Of the millions of blogs that exist in cyberspace, there are those that will never reach anyone; they will exist in anonymity for some time and finally falter, unmissed and unloved, the non-cyborg step-sisters of the mommyblogs who are outside of the interactivity of the mamasphere. Particularly for very isolated mothers (those with very young children, large families, or nonmainstream social or physical locations) the need for community is dramatic: to tell the story and have no one respond, then, could be devastating. If the relationality of the mamasphere provides validation and support, the absence of that support can be potentially traumatic, and the discourse is then shifted to the quest for comments rather than being focused on the comments themselves.

A variety of techniques are used by mommybloggers to ensure readership. For example, a commitment to "linky love" or reciprocal linking to other blogs almost immediately directs traffic towards blogs; likewise, commenting on lots of other mommyblogs ensures that traffic is directed back to the source. Posts that end in questions specifically directed towards commenters tend to garner higher numbers of comments; while fishing for feedback, this technique nonetheless creates a cyborg communality that seems to portray a high level of sincerity, since substantive comments are required in response to the original post. More crass attempts to gain popularity include the increasingly controversial "search engine optimization," which inspires bloggers to ensure that their own blog name appears in the maximum number of links, thereby ensuring a higher Google or Technorati page rank. In addition, bloggers may be exceedingly calculating about which words to focus on within posts and titles to ensure that their site is as likely as possible to garner traffic from search engines.

One unsubtle example comes from Tara of *The Young Mommy Life*: "Folks are always searching for cute maternity clothes. Every day several people find my site after typing in phrases like 'maternity clothes that won't make me look old' or 'pregnant woman desires cute clothes.'"[18]

By highlighting the terms often used to seek information, Tara ensures that her site will be reached easily by anyone entering these terms into a search engine. These terms are far from random, however. Instead, these terms draw on conventional ideas about appropriate motherhood and the links between mothering and consumerism.

These techniques alter the narrative of mommyblogs. Yet these methods are not without power in themselves: in few other contexts are the keys to popularity (or at least visibility) so explicit. For mothers who may experience a lack of control in other aspects of their lives, controlling the narrative provides a unique power, even as the traditional autobiographical contract is abrogated, or at least adhered to less sincerely.[19] At the same time, the distinct personal connection – the cyborg – that characterizes the most consistently popular mommyblogs tends to vanish in these constrained attempts at readership: readers may pass by, may comment, even, but in this context actual community remains as elusive online as it may be in real life. This places mommybloggers in a bind: sincerity may be rewarded with community, but it may also leave women vulnerable to receiving hateful comments. More strategic postings can yield the illusion of popularity but do not provide intimacy. Yet in this dichotomy power is once again unmasked as both complicated and diffuse, in that mothers have the capacity both to author the story and to control its dissemination.

In looking at the ways that mommybloggers experience authorial power by and against the cyborg, examples of power's true complexity emerge. Power's performance within the non-star mamasphere is the opposite of Bentham's panopticon: rather than being centrally realized and a product of focused scrutiny, unknown mommyblogs confront the power wielded by a *lack* of scrutiny (Winokur, 2003). Bloggers participate in a constant negotiation of power between creator and audience that references other sites of power (the power of dominant narratives of motherhood, as well as the specific constraints/opportunities of the medium) but do not present an ordered hierarchy. In the disruptions and confusion of the mamasphere, the fissures and discontinuities of power are exposed and, at best, exploited in order to disrupt hierarchies of oppression that are born of normative expectations. This disorder is evident in considering the ways that popularity and power are enacted within the writing of star mommybloggers.

"Whuffie": Popular Mommybloggers

If unknown bloggers experience the reverse of panopticism in their general lack of scrutiny, popular mommybloggers reverse the trend yet again. The popular bloggers selected for this study[20] did not come to fame prior to blogging; rather, all are now well known within certain circles because of their blogging prowess and their capacity to access the cyborg. They have specifically found success in the mamasphere by virtue of their access to an indescribable something often referred to as "whuffie." Science fiction writer Cory Doctorow presents a future world wherein monetary value is replaced by a different currency: recognition. Whuffie, then, refers to reputation-based currency, a system in which prestige may lead to the acquisition of material goods (Doctorow, 2003). Scott Rosenberg (2009) writes that "Doctorow's readers immediately understood that he was describing a kind of value that already existed in the Web's cross-linked conversations" (p. 202).

The intangible effects of success within a web-based society that are manifested in whuffie have been translated into more traditional rewards such as popularity and monetary success for bloggers who possess this characteristic. The whuffie of popular mommyblogs presents a different type of cyborg relationality, in that readers are not simply a shared community but are instead a more traditional audience. Furthermore, this growth in readership generally emerges stealthily and organically, such that popular mommybloggers may have made the shift from community to audience both unintentionally and without immediate notice. This presents specific opportunities and challenges to star mommybloggers.

The popular bloggers of this study are, as discussed in chapter 3, generally normative. As white, educated, and relatively class-privileged mothers in heterosexual marriages, they do not begin to represent the full diversity of the mamasphere. At the same time, however, these mothers are drawing attention specifically because the stories they tell are so desperately unlike the standard maternal story and, perhaps as a result, present an unmasked motherhood hungry for community. Popular mommybloggers are angry about the limitations and constraints of patriarchal motherhood and have translated this characteristic into whuffie. In participating so completely within the mamasphere, they have also created cyborg selves, and they have done this by inventing popular online personae who are kept "alive" and reinvented through a huge body of writing spanning, in each case, more than five years of regular posts.

Star mommybloggers bring many of the theories of motherhood studies to life. These are illustrated in bite-sized examples from their own lives and the lives of mothers around them, and thus they are used to begin conversations that spin off into comments and other blogs. Yet none of the popular bloggers discussed here began by assuming they would achieve great popularity and success, and all of them have found that the scrutiny of their popularity has potentially limited their capacity to be critical of traditional motherhood. Alice Bradley of *Finslippy* makes this point:

> It's hard to put yourself out there. Some days it's harder than others, of course, but there's always a risk that you're going to get a negative reaction to what you've written. You can't anticipate what will set some stranger off on a tear about how much you suck. It doesn't get easier, either; once you get some experience under your belt, you start to anticipate the reactions to whatever it is you're writing. You imagine the people who aren't that into you reading it and smirking. They're like your Inner Critic come to life – a whole Greek chorus of voices telling the world how overrated you are. And then you stop yourself from writing, or you tell yourself you need more time, more inspiration, more something. That's letting fear win, and by winning, it gets stronger, and the feeling snowballs. Pretty soon you're also imagining all the people who think you suck because you don't post enough. And then you've locked yourself in a closet and you're wearing tissue boxes for shoes. It's not healthy, kids.[21]

Alice's comments are not wildly different from those articulated by less popular bloggers, but as a "star" mommyblogger, she faces a much greater degree of scrutiny, coupled with a lesser degree of connection with her readers, since she cannot possibly follow the blogs of all of her followers. Yet, while she confesses her insecurities, Alice nonetheless continues to share intimate details of her mental health struggles and difficult parenting decisions – despite no longer languishing in either anonymity or obscurity. Her readers have come to find community with one another (I have had lengthy conversations with strangers in which we bond over the latest post on *Finslippy*) and she continues to bravely present her truths despite the challenges of questioning mainstream motherhood in such a public context. Furthermore, Alice, like all the star bloggers examined here, continues to value the process of analysing motherhood in the cyborg community context, even if the dialogue is at arm's length and presents a less explicitly interactive format. These blogs thus capitalize on the capacity of the mamasphere to allow laypeople to begin to demystify the expectations and limitations of motherhood.

The pitfalls of public online mothering and popularity are epitomized by Heather of *Dooce*. *Dooce*'s influence extends far beyond the realm of the mamasphere; Heather was listed among *Forbes* magazine's thirty most influential women in media for 2009. Like Alice, Heather is both witty and irreverent; she has also documented her personal ordeal with a serious postpartum depression following the birth of her older daughter, Leta. Heather's commitment to telling her own story extended to her handwriting blog posts, uploaded by her partner, from a mental hospital. While *Dooce* exposes, in raw detail, some of the most silenced aspects of new motherhood, the blog's popularity has come at a price for Heather. When her commenters created a thriving and interactive community in the comments of her daily posts, the numbers reached hundreds, sometimes even thousands. Because of the high number of negative comments interspersed with community-building, Heather chose to close comments on most posts, effectively shutting down an organic community in order to protect herself and her family. She writes,

> I had to take a small step back and remember just why I am doing this, why the hell do I continue to do this when people say horrible things about me on my own website, horrible things about me on other people's websites, horrible things about my innocent daughter or my husband or anyone that I love.[22]

On the one hand, Heather is arguably one of the most powerful personal bloggers of all time, the quintessential cyborg mother. Her website, full of musings, has become such a successful advertising vehicle that it is now a successful business employing her, her partner, and several other employees. Her influence is vast: at the present moment more than one million people are following her on Twitter and a brief mention of a trend in one of Heather's posts leads to a tremendous surge in traffic and attention towards websites and products. Given her celebrity, it is perhaps unsurprising that she is on the receiving end of such negativity. The nature of her popularity, however, has ensured that the nature of the criticism focuses on her "whoring"

or "pimping" her children – both extremely troubling gendered met-
aphors that are not used accidentally. *Dooce's* detractors frequently
bemoan how boring Heather has become since having children (and
here "mommyblog" is used as an epithet); in comments and emails,
certain readers seem to feel that if Heather can discuss her children
online, everyone else may do so as well and refer to her children in
deeply unflattering terms (manifesting one of the chief pitfalls of a
cyborg relationality). Heather is equally maligned as a mother and a
blogger, as in the following excerpt:

> I am tired of her bullying attitude and the how-dare-anyone-say-any-
> thing-bad-about-me – THE ALMIGHTY DOOCE! Yeah, get over your-
> self – you're a blogger. Not a nurse, not a teacher, not a therapist . . . not
> anyone who has devoted their life to actually helping people. You're a
> self-serving mother who is pouring your children's lives all over the Inter-
> net for the sake of Target/Ikea/etsy crap. I can guaran-frickin-tee she isn't
> giving ANY money to charity. Unless it is for the Foundation for Mor-
> mon Transvestites with Deformed Chins. Or the Society of Mommies who
> Deny their Kids have Autism.[23]

Heather has provided several examples of creative and hilarious
ways to capitalize on her negative publicity. In the fall of 2009, she
launched a new feature of *Dooce* – "Monetizing The Hate." She meticu-
lously posted all negative comments and emails, such as the example
shown above, as well as a huge number of ads. Every time someone
provided more fodder for this component of the site, they put money
in *Dooce's* coffers. Earlier in the same year, Heather took her private
frustrations with a broken (and brand-new) washing machine public,
tweeting about her experiences and repeatedly exhorting her one million followers to avoid Maytag products. While she received a riot of
negative attention following this move, she also got her washer fixed
and a second washer (which she donated to a local women's shelter)
given to her almost instantaneously.

In looking at *Dooce*, the diffuse nature of power is visible: financial power is achieved, as is popularity, but the exposure that comes
with popularity opens Heather up to public excoriation. The success
of monetization comes with an obligation to constantly provide more:
more posts, more bells and whistles, more features, and more humour.
In this respect, Heather cannot be easily seen as powerful or powerless, but rather as an example of the complicated and contradictory

nature of power. Power can be seen as calculated, however, in the very sexist and anti-maternal rhetoric that is aimed at the site. While Heather arguably faces the same degree of criticism as any other celebrity, the nature of that criticism is targeted at her as a mother – specifically, as a mother who has had the audacity to suggest that her unmasking of motherhood is worthy of attention and scrutiny. At the same time, there are legions of women who point to Heather's prose as literally life-saving in its exposure of postpartum depression and mental health challenges. Furthermore, Heather has realized the extent to which her popularity is dependent on a cyborg approach: her readership diminished in the absence of open comments and, in response, she has now created an online *Dooce* community in which commenters can respond to her and one another in a moderated context.

Dooce is now an enterprise, but an enterprise with motherhood at its centre, and Heather can thus be seen as masterfully exploiting her location at the centre of a relational maternal medium through which she responds to the inaccuracies and limitations of dominant motherhood discourse. Whuffie is a complex form of relationality, one that may have more in common with more traditional understandings of audience and author. Nonetheless, in drawing its roots from the cyborg, the whuffie of star mommybloggers like Heather presents an interesting and complex response to traditional motherhood.

When traditional media analyse the mamasphere, they tend to focus on star mommyblogs and those with greater readership. Yet to do so is to undermine the very cyborg nature of the mamasphere and the intense relationality of "average" mommyblogs. While many mothers read *Dooce*, *Finslippy*, and the others, most of those readers are also engaged in complex and unfolding relationships with one another. While it is important to look towards star mommybloggers, it is equally important to remember that they are ultimately the mamasphere's aberrations and that the true power of mommyblogs rests in the power of multiple voices, not the few who speak loudest. Returning to Hayles (2006), the impact of the mamasphere's multiplicity – characterized by Hayles as the "cognisphere" – is much more potent than the behaviour of its stars. Hayles argues that

> The cognisphere takes up where the cyborg left off. No longer bound in a binary with the goddess but rather emblem and instantiation of dynamic cognitive flows between human, animal and machine, the cognisphere,

like the world itself, is not binary but multiple, not a split creature but a co-evolving and densely interconnected complex system. (p. 165)

In order to adequately understand that complex and organic system, I now turn to one of its chief cyborg characteristics – the mamasphere's dynamic relationship with temporality.

On Temporality

The machine age has led to a greater organic connectivity independent of time and physical place. By using computers to literally form a network, mothers are quilting an exquisite and exhaustive picture of their lives. While it is always tempting to talk of this archive as an artefact for future generations, to do so ignores the lack of temporality of the mamasphere. As it unravels before us, the future generation is already being blogged about and, in some cases, seamlessly taking on blogging as they move forward. The cyborg mamasphere is thus a tough new fabric unrolling before us; not a red carpet for future generations to follow, but instead a network of bridges woven between us, connecting mothers across time.

While infertility blogger Julie of *A Little Pregnant* now has two sons, women who are currently struggling with infertility, as she did in the past, can find solace in her archives. Furthermore, in her present-day reflections, Julie refers to women online who are currently in the midst of the struggles of infertility. Many mothers have suggested that the simple ability to find mothers who are experiencing any given stage of mothering builds important connections – even if a particular mother experienced that stage five years ago and a reader can only relate to that experience in the blogger's archive. These connections are deeply cyborg for two key reasons: they maximize the relationship between organisms and technology (between mother and blog) and they connect each individual blogger back to her former self while empowering her with the capacity to choose which moments and texts will get the most attention moving into the future. Through comments, even retrospective ones, by-gone discussions can be resurrected and examined through the lens of present/future knowledge. Julie comments on this ability to time-travel:

A couple of days ago I got a comment on an old post, as I occasionally do. These always intrigue me; it's like some weird inverted Moebius wormholey time-capsule Wayback thing. Sometimes I answer, if it seems a sincere and urgent question has been asked, but usually those comments just sit there, three or four years after the initial post and its comments. *Someone was wrong on the Internet! There's proof right here in the fossil record!*[24]

A discussion of the temporality of the cyborg mamasphere once again presents mommyblogs as dynamic entities that are not always performing at the exclusive behest of their authors.

Reflecting on some difficult parenting choices, Briar from *Unwellness* describes the blog as a "blessing that holds delicious memory and as [a] record that keeps bringing up the hard stuff."[25] Briar begins by looking at the mundane event of having just received an unexpected and very old medical bill. She reflects on how she used her blog as a means of establishing what was occurring at the time that the medical procedure in question was meant to have taken place. This reflection is both instrumentally effective in empowering her to successfully challenge her insurance provider, but also emotionally unsettling as she is unsuspectingly plunged into the difficult terrain of a miscarriage suffered several years prior. Yet such use of personal narrative is not necessarily distinct from the way any given mother might write about a similar ordeal in an offline private diary. What allows the specific temporal characteristics of mommyblogs to disrupt dominant motherhood?

On a practical level, mommyblogs do not expose the interruptions that are so endemic to parenting young children; instead, they provide a visually seamless recounting of mothers' experiences at this stage. While the actual writing of any given post might be riddled with interruption, the post that is left behind possesses a coherence that is a product of technology. Furthermore, in tandem with the cyborg relationality of the mamasphere, mommyblogs allow mothers to post stories from which conversations can emerge in their absence. It is thus the combination of the unending structure of mommyblogs and their dialogism that characterizes their cyborg nature. These attributes are coupled with the use of technology to create deliberately self-referential narratives and links between blogs.

Linking allows for a richness in the narrative that transcends time. This is true across the blogosphere, but is distinctly understood in the realm of motherhood. As mothers of young children know, each distinct parenting stage is fleeting and is never as memorable as one might assume. More important, however, is the extent to which mothers are born and evolve alongside their young children. By encouraging dialogue with earlier parenting selves, mommyblogs allow for an un-precedented self-reflection. Furthermore, as participants in the mom-myblogging community, readers can access the full archive of parenting experience that exists online, rather than simply the mothering wisdom of any given mother at any given present moment. Mommyblogs thus use technology to transcend time as well as physical space.

The cyborg mommyblogger benefits from the ceaselessness of blog-ging's methodology but, in her interactions with that method, she can also shift time itself. Mommybloggers can return to earlier texts and manipulate, edit, or delete them. This ability to tinker maintains a spirit of flexibility and reflection that is a refreshing antidote to the fixed and unyielding strictures of expert discourses of motherhood. For example, Laura of *Florida Girl in Sydney* writes at the end of a particular post: "Update: June 30th – I hate this blog posting. I may delete it soon. Up-date July 22nd – Still thinking about it."[26] As Deborah Bowen (2009) reminds us,

> These are open spaces, inherently public by their very medium. The para-dox of this public private space is as follows: the author has the power within that space to reveal – or not reveal! – that which is most pressing in her mind. The "room of her own" is ultimately a combination of her Web-space and her own mind. (p. 314)

The mamasphere thus presents a composite of millions of mothers who are changing the way mothering is presented in the public view, as well as a composite of any given mother in her past, present, and fu-ture voice. Such a practice draws heavily on more traditional forms of life writing, especially diaries and journals, but extends the capacity for self-reflection born of an analogue age and its methods through the tools of this machine age.

The mamasphere emerges as a highly unfixed space, a "narrative ex-hibiting some features of narrativity, some of which may indeed be de-ferred, fragmentary, or disunifying" (Kadar, 1992, p. 159). When they play with time, subject, view, and other conventions, mommybloggers are also disrupting conventions of motherhood. Bowen (2009), writing about the online diaries that prefigured blogs, argues, "The online au-tobiography has the potential to be a safe environment for women . . . here, women can articulate bodies of knowledge based on their own experiences and perceptions, and in so doing, subvert and redefine ex-tant discourses" (p. 311). Bowen credits the interactive and fast-moving nature of virtual reading and writing with allowing possibilities that traditional autobiographical spaces do not. The specific cyborg temporality is clearly central to this new autobiographical and polyvocal space. The speed with which mommybloggers can react to one another (as well as to parenting news within the world at large) creates an immediacy and a freshness that, coupled with a capacity to enter past stories virtually instantly, presents a powerful response to notions of mothering as a fixed and unyielding enterprise. Mommyblogs are thus both reflective because they can look into the past and immediate because they have the capacity to instantaneously react to trends and narratives written in the present moment.

In her "cyborg momifesto," Bon writes,

> the cyborg mother, of course, ought to be a contradiction in terms. the mother image is organic, the original origin story. but the cyborg is contradiction embodied. and the cyborg mother lives firmly in the postdigital age that the voices of doom and essentialistic difference do not realize has reached us. the digital age is as much a part of us as the technology of the telephone or the pencil. we have incorporated it into ourselves – our baby monitors, our Dr. Google, our youtube videos of our children or for our children, our networks of identity and friendship and expression and marketing. who we make of ourselves as a result will be different from the mothers we grew up with, indeed, as will our children be different from the 70s and 80s versions of self we once were.[27]

The disruption of time and space can create potentially uncomfortable effects, especially in the context of disturbing narratives found online. In writing this book, I may "finish" reading a blog for my research but I know the blogger is depressed, and I know that her post about depression was written this morning as I dropped my children off at school. As I document her archive, this blogger may well be out there, in Tokyo or Des Moines or Lancashire, facing uncertainty and difficulty. The open-endedness of mommyblogging has led to an awkwardness in my scholarship, since I always want to hear the next installment of any given mommyblogging story. This is both overwhelming and exhilarating – the fact that the story literally never ends – again, in a way quite distinct from other autobiographical forms, even diaries that are eventually shared and/or published – is troubling to my own sense of narrative arc. While I have read innumerable offline diaries and memoirs, I have only seen them in published form, after the story has been edited and neatly tied off. Nonetheless, it is in this disruption that I see critical challenges posed to dominant discourses of motherhood; in the ephemerality and open-endedness of mommyblogging, no one parenting "truth" can be concretized into fact and thus the slippery confusion of mothering is exposed and affirmed.

The View from Everywhere? Temporality, the Author, and the Authored

Barthes (1977) suggests that "to give a text an author is to impose a limit on that text, to furnish it with a final signified, to close the writing" (para. 7). Can the cyborg mother act as the anti-Author and, instead, open the possibilities of writing? How does the genre of blogging allow this possibility? Obviously, as discussed above, the relationality of blogging allows for unprecedented collectivity in authorship, a complex dialogue in place of a foreclosed narrative. Yet it is not simply the relationality of mommyblogs that allows for their open structure. Diaries are both self-referential and open-ended, but are often kept private. Furthermore, for the majority of diaries kept in handwritten form, access to past narratives would have been limited by an inability to easily search through the writing. In her work, Elizabeth Podnieks (2004) shows that although diaries were often shared with family and friends and sometimes even written with publication in mind, many remained private; even diaries that were shared would suffer from a relatively limited audience while those that were published would have had a temporally imposed end point.

In traditional memoirs in Barthes's terms, the writing is limited by a traditional narrative structure and eventually comes to an end. In sharp contrast, as discussed above, blogs evolve, are immediate, and have no temporal limits. The writing is open-ended and the signifying that occurs is shifted towards possibility, away from definitive conclusions. The mamasphere is constantly inventing and being invented, shifting and evolving in contrast to static writing about Good Mothers found in expert texts. Instead, the mothers presented online are like quicksilver, presenting a range of mothering practices that are difficult to pin down. They are sassy, multifaceted, diverse, and so much more dynamic than their analogue counterparts. In short, mommyblogs represent the constant negotiation and diversity of mothers from the inside out. These mothers reject the institution of motherhood and are more consistent with the work of mothering, with its messiness, inconsistency, and infinite details; they present a matrifocal narrative that extends the earlier life writings by mothers and amplifies these writings greatly. The fluid temporality of the cyborg mamasphere contributes to the destabilization of dominant discourses of motherhood by allowing for these evolving and multifarious maternal accounts to proliferate and to be continuously refreshed.

As each individual maternal subject writes her truth, she does not do so in isolation; the relationality discussed earlier creates a composite model of maternity that responds to a need to unmask motherhood. In responding to other blogs and to her own comments, backward and forward in time, the mother/author begins to participate in a collective autobiography that is richer than its individual parts. In order to understand the collective maternal subject, then, I now turn to a consideration of the collective cyborg.

The Multidimensional Cyborg: The Mamasphere's Collective Mother

If, as *Her Bad Mother* blogger Catherine asserts, "the blogging mothers have created a new kind of motherhood," then how can this new kind of motherhood be characterized? What possibilities does this new motherhood offer? Most importantly, can the seeds of a new collective view of motherhood be sown in the relationality and alternate temporality of the mamasphere, in the cyborg nature of the mommyblog? If the patriarchal discourse of motherhood presents a stereotypical and unrealistic emblematic mother, is there a collective alternate subject emerging in the cumulative subjectivities of millions of mothers online?

On the subject of collectives, feminist scholar, author, and activist Minnie Bruce Pratt writes, "I am speaking my small piece of truth, as best I can . . . I'm putting it down for you to see if our fragments match anywhere, if our pieces, together, make another larger piece of the truth that can be part of the map we are making together to show us the way to get to the longed-for world" (quoted in Smith & Watson, 1998, p. 189). Pratt suggests that transformative change is a possibility drawn from the creation of collective stories such as those seen in the mamasphere. Motherhood sorely needs precisely such a transformative change.

Blogger Alison writes on her blog *Et Al.* about one such collectivity: "First of all, thanks to those of you who have sent emails and posted kind words. This 'virtual' community feels pretty darned real to me."[28] Alison writes about her life as an academic mother and as caregiver to her husband who eventually passes away from cancer. Along with other bloggers in similar circumstances, Alison refers to herself as a member in "The Saddest Club Ever." The women in this "club" – young widows raising young children – have found solace and community and have comforted one another, fundraised for each other and otherwise provided support that any community would be proud to offer. Yet, as discussed in chapter 3, what is interesting is that their commonality does not undermine their significant differences. While they are all widows, they put forth a composite maternal narrative of single motherhood, working life, and the mundane frustrations of parenting small children and keeping a household running. Their blogs share commonalities with other blogs across the web: blogger Snickollet underwent assisted reproductive technology to conceive before her partner died and thus sought out other mommybloggers in similar circumstances; Alison is as much a presence within academic mommyblogs as within the tightly knit circle of "The Saddest Club." It is, therefore, hard to get a reading on what "the mamasphere presents." There are multiple mamaspheres, and mommybloggers hop in and out of each realm with true cyborg impunity, thus creating different, non-normative collective mother-subjects.

These multiple mamaspheres hearken back to the collective biographies that consider affinities of groups of people and organize biography into identity categories in response. In stark contrast, however, the identity categories of the multiple cyborg collectivities of the mamasphere are unfixed and pliant and mommybloggers may participate in many such groups simultaneously. By threatening fixed notions of both maternal practice and non-normative social locations, the cyborg mother that emerges in the collective autobiography of mothers online thus presents an important alternative to dominant discourses of motherhood. Extending Pratt's analysis to the arena of motherhood where the emblematic Mother is so oppressive a figure, this collective storytelling could create an alternate picture of mothers that focuses on different traits, skills, and fears than the mother articulated by the dominant discourse of motherhood.

Julie of *Geisha School Dropout* writes about motherhood, her Korean-American identity, bisexuality, and innumerable other topics of interest to her and her readers. Her irreverent style and breezy wit have made her quite popular. She writes about going to a convention of Asian-American bloggers (titled BANANA, it took place at the University of Southern California in November 2009), and posts this musing after the fact:

When it was over, I was replenished with a sense of awe at the possibility and promise of my generation of Asian Americans that I had lost in my college years. Maybe it was the specific people around me at the time, but I just thought my colleagues were just content to become personally successful and not really sweat it about making a bigger impact, but my fellow panelists proved me wrong. It made me wish I knew them back then, and a bit wistful at the lost opportunity. But hey, I ain't dead yet; if any of them need a helping hand, I'll definitely offer one, albeit one covered in baby shit.[29]

Julie presents herself as both an insider in the Asian-American community and in the mothering community. Significantly, however, she seems to feel somewhat awkward about blending the two; she is "the mommyblogger" at the convention and thus distinct from other Asian-American bloggers without children; within the mamasphere she is an *Asian-American* mother, rather than simply "mainstream." Yet, along with great numbers of other Asian-American mommybloggers, she is contributing (singly and through sites like *Kimchi Mamas*) to a distinct cyborg mother-narrative that has found its own niche within the broader world of mommyblogging. While sometimes these distinct mamaspheres appear to be ghettos, the fluidity with which mommybloggers navigate between their own different subjectivities is unprecedented and therefore allows entry into, and the constant re-constitution of, multiple mamaspheres. These multiple mamaspheres are a mixed blessing: they may lack the political power of "the mainstream" (and, indeed, require critical reflection on this term, since the mamasphere itself is far from mainstream), but at the same time they allow mothers of different and multiple affinities and identities to seek each other out and begin to interrupt dominant discourses of motherhood that have always excluded them. The blogger behind *Typical American Mom*, for instance, describes her blog as "Reflections from the harried life of a 'typical American' Chicagoland mom of three young boys, if you want to call a midlife, second-generation Korean American typical . . . which I do, actually!"[30]

The discursive construction of millions of mothers through their blogs has led to the cyborg mother-subject being constructed as her own complicated and multi-faceted entity. If the dominant discourse of motherhood is about certainty and simplicity in the form of proscriptions, the collective subject that is created by the mamasphere is about contradictions and convolutions. This dynamism is reminiscent of VNS

Matrix's (1991) notion of the "common cunt": the emergence of a subject that has historically been viewed as monolithic and singular somehow becoming a common, shared creation. Susan Stanford Friedman (1988) considers this commonality as central to women's life writing: "In taking the power of words, of representation, into their own hands, women project onto history an identity that is not purely individualistic. Nor is it purely collective. Instead, this new identity merges the shared and the unique" (p. 76).

Bronwyn Davies and Susanne Gannon (2006) write of their own experiences with collective autobiography:

> We talk the talk around our memories, the listening to the detail of each other's memories, as a technology for enabling us to produce, through attention to the embodied sense of being in the remembered moment, a truth in relation to what cannot actually be recovered – the moment as it was lived. This is not a naïve, naturalistic truth, but a truth that is worked on through a technology of telling, listening and writing. In a sense it is the very *unreliability* of memory that allows this close discursive work. (p. 3)

As Davies and Gannon describe it here, collective autobiography is a fundamentally cyborg enterprise. In creating a polyvocal and shifting representation, knowledge creation becomes a process rather than a fixed goal. This is consistent with the unspooling and evolving knowledge that mothers create online.

Bowen (2009) argues that "finally, the combination of genre and medium – the diary and the Web, in this case – permit the genesis of this new discursive tradition" (p. 311). She asks women to embrace a new tradition, replacing *écriture féminine* (feminine writing) with "*e-criture féminine*" – a new cyber method of women's writing:

> The difference between *écriture* and *e-criture* is the difference between solipsism and collectivism. While any woman is free to engage in life writing from/of herself, the discourse that *e-criture* helps to encourage allows women to write individually *and* as part of a burgeoning group. (2009, p. 324)

Our collective Mother is the repository for the burgeoning group, the author of the collective subjectivity. Her story is an important counter-narrative to that of the presentation of patriarchal motherhood, infinitely richer and more diverse, more critical and equally more optimistic, open to a dramatic array of possibilities. These possibilities are realized in the many corners of the mamasphere that might themselves be characterized as separate spaces, as mamaspheres from the margins.

While the relationality, unusual temporality, and collectivity of the mamasphere are presented here as distinct characteristics of mommyblogs, it is, of course, the congruency of these various cyborg characteristics that build the mamasphere, despite the many normative maternal accounts contained therein, as a potentially radical medium. The emergent dialogism and immediacy of the mamasphere allow for a collective picture of maternity to emerge that is stubbornly difficult to capture but that, in its elusiveness, presents a useful and credible threat to mainstream maternal accounts. Looking more closely at the specific interactivity of technology and motherhood, however, could provide insight into the instability of the maternal subject and the potential destabilization of subjectivity as a whole. These ideas are now explored in the framework of queer theory.

5 On Queer: A Liminal and Unfixed Motherhood

Was I the mother who baked? Who took her kid to McDonalds? Who knew the words to nursery rhymes? Who snubbed children's activities as not cool enough? Who was sexy? Who didn't buy into the whole yummy mummy thing? Who flirted? Who didn't think about sex anymore? Who used cloth nappies or disposables? Who cared about what nappies other people were using? Who talks about renovations? Who compares their children's colds? Who booked her child into a private school at birth? Who hadn't thought about school yet? Who forgot her child's lunch at the playground? Who wouldn't let her daughter wear pink? Who dressed her daughter and herself in the same outfits? Who shouted at her child? Who got a headache from not shouting at her child? Who called herself "Lauca's Mum"? Who drank too much? Who wouldn't touch a drop in front of her child? Who laughed at cartoons? Who couldn't stand children's TV? Who did art and craft sessions with her child? Who wouldn't have glue on her floors? Who used flash cards? Who thought it was all such a wank?

– *Blue Milk*[1]

If hybridity allows for an analysis of the breadth and diversity of the mamasphere, and the cyborg gives consideration to the relationality and dialogic nature of mommyblogging, what insight may be gained by considering the mamasphere through the lens of queer theory? Drawing from Judith Halberstam's (2005) assertion that a "queer adjustment" (p. 6) allows for opportunities to reconsider ideas of both time and space, is it possible to view mothers who blog with this queer adjustment in mind?

Fundamentally, a queer analysis of motherhood allows for an unfixed subjectivity to emerge. Such an understanding draws from Patti Lather's (1991) suggestion that "remarks *toward* a definition be used to displace the desire to comprehend, to 'clearly understand'" (p. 5). If our approach to motherhood is against understanding, rather than an attempt to trap a fixed notion of the maternal subject, then a queer reading has much to offer. Indeed, to return to the term's origins (to be discussed in detail below), a "queer" view of motherhood would explicitly allow for an unusual or peculiar motherhood to emerge, one that is notable for its lack of normalcy rather than its adherence to an evolved or shifted new positionality. This new motherhood would exist between current understandings, allowing for the emergence of a *liminal* motherhood: one that is not wholly any one thing but instead lies between fixed positions.

There are many possible approaches to take in considering a queer view of motherhood and the liminality of the maternal subject. Chapter 3 began to consider the ways that varied maternal practices and identities threaten a stable maternal identity while chapter 4 looked at the implications of mothers in dialogue and in relation to one another online. These earlier analyses point towards a shift or disruption of the stable maternal subject in the mamasphere. To arrive at a "full" reckoning of a queer motherhood, however, requires a consideration of the ways that motherhood itself can be seen as a threat to the enterprise of stable identity construction. By acknowledging the ways that queer identity has destabilized the whole notion of stability itself, we may find similar implications for a close examination of motherhood (and the specific site of mommyblogs) in shifting analyses of identity construction beyond the realm of the individual subject towards, instead, a contextualized and relational selfhood.

The mother who blogs at *Front Porch* considers this relational selfhood as the intensity of her mothering shifts with her youngest child, Connor, attending school for the first time:

> Connor in school means that I will be home alone. ALONE. Which is truly strange. I have mixed feelings about it. I'm excited to have this bit of freedom, but I also feel like I'm losing a part of myself. Who am I if I don't have Connor following me everywhere?[2]

While this blogger uses the anonymity of blogging to tell her own story, she does not refer to herself at all in her blog, even by pseudonym. As a result, she is simply "Connor and Maddy's mother"; as her life begins to shift away from the ceaseless caregiving of early parenthood she must begin to consider who she is as an individual again. A relational approach to motherhood asks not only who this mother is as she renegotiates an individual subjectivity, but who she was during the period of intense conjoinment when her own selfhood was indelibly wed to that of her children. This analysis positions queer motherhood as antithetical to an individualistic discourse through an examination of the intense conjoinment of mothers and their children.

In order to understand the implications of a queer reading of mommyblogs, this chapter will begin by examining the genesis of the term "queer" as well as its political importance within gay/lesbian studies and activism. Having established the relevance of the term, I will consider a queer perspective on the mamasphere, examining the ways that a queer view of motherhood through mommyblogs may enrich an understanding of the maternal subject and subjectivity as a whole. The chapter will end with a consideration of the implications of a fractured and performative maternal subjectivity for children.

History of Queer Theory

Queer theory was coined as a phrase by Teresa de Lauretis in her 1990 talk (and subsequent article) with this signal phrase as its name (Halperin, 2003, p. 339). De Lauretis (1991) suggested that queer theory allows us "to recast or reinvent the terms of our sexualities, to construct another discursive horizon, another way of thinking the sexual" (p. iv).

While de Lauretis may have been the scholar to initially put forth the phrase, "queer theory" is widely understood to have had many different points of origin beyond this original writing, each contributing something different to its key theme – an insistence on the *non-normative* as central. This rejection of normativity has resulted in one of the theory's more challenging attributes: a fundamental resistance to definition. The website theory.org.uk explicitly links this characteristic to the slipperiness of subjectivity, suggesting that

> it is a mistake to think that queer theory is another name for lesbian and gay studies. They're different. Queer theory *has something to say to* lesbian and gay studies – and also to a bunch of other areas of sociology and cultural theory . . . Queer theory is a set of ideas based around the idea that identities are not fixed and do not determine who we are. It suggests that it is meaningless to talk in general about "women" or any other group, as identities consist of so many elements that to assume that people can be seen collectively on the basis of one shared characteristic is wrong. Indeed, it proposes that we deliberately challenge all notions of fixed identity, in varied and non-predictable ways.[3]

This reading, suggesting that queer identity is in flux, discursively constructed, and volatile, began as a means of understanding the limitations
of identity politics within the GLBT community. From its inception in
the late 1960s, the gay rights movement generally did not acknowledge
lesbian subjectivity; bisexuals were often left out of the discourse; and
the eventual inclusion of transgendered people to the acronym, and the
movement, did not necessarily lead to a productive dialogue about the
needs and desires of people who were trans and intersex. In the multiplicity of "queer," then, identity politics began to fail. As a result, GLBT
activists and academics had two choices: they could expand the acronym
and look for multiplicity through an acknowledgment of further areas
of difference, or they could repatriate an existing term and use it as an
open-ended umbrella for the widest possible range of people.[4]

While the choice to embrace the word queer came from its historical positioning as an epithet applied to gays and lesbians, it is important to consider the implications of this particular terminology. Unlike
other reclaimed identity markers, queer, defined as odd or unusual, is
notable for its lack of description. Someone who is queer is someone
who is outside the norm, rather than a person who is described in his
or her own right. On the one hand, this term can thus be seen as a form
of debasement – people described as queer do not even have the right
to their own descriptor, but are rather only seen in terms of an unflattering comparison. On the other hand, however, the term itself is politically brilliant in its capacity to open, rather than foreclose, possibilities:
fundamentally, the only definition of someone who is queer is someone who is, on some level, not "normal." Thus, the specific characteristics that comprise any given subject's lack of normality are left unfixed,
open to infinite possibilities. This reading returns to de Lauretis's position: she begins with a specific analysis that focuses on sexuality as
a site of difference, but ultimately does so in a way that foregrounds
openness and possibility rather than fixed identity categories. Within
her three tenets of the theory in its infancy, she looks towards the intersectionality of sexuality with race (which can presumably be extended
equally to other characteristics of social location); the lack of fixity
within sexual identity itself; and an openness to resisting the hegemony
of heterosexuality as the norm from which individuals deviate.

Highlighting the challenges of truly working within a deconstructive
notion of identity, de Lauretis abandoned the term three years after
she initially coined it, arguing that the term had been appropriated by

precisely the mainstream institutions that it sought to critique. By that time, Judith Butler's *Gender Trouble* and Eve Kosofsky Sedgwick's *Epistemology of the Closet* had continued the theoretical work undertaken by de Lauretis. Writing about gender, rather than sexuality, Butler (1990) wrote,

> Is the construction of the category of women as a coherent and stable subject an unwitting regulation and reification of gender relations? And is not such a reification precisely contrary to feminist aims? To what extent does the category of women achieve stability and coherence only in the context of the heterosexual matrix? If a stable notion of gender no longer proves to be the foundational premise of feminist politics, perhaps a new sort of feminist politics is now desirable to contest the very reification of gender and identity, one that will take the variable construction of identity as both a methodological and normative prerequisite, if not a political goal. (p. 9)

While Butler focuses on the central political importance of "variable construction of identity," Sedgwick takes a slightly different approach. Looking at the history of the institution of homosexuality, Sedgwick asks how such a wide range of practices, desires, and characteristics have come to be subsumed under such limited and limiting terminology. As an alternative, she suggests that we must consider a reading of sex and desire that is merely *descriptive* rather than *prescriptive*. Such a reading invites the questions put forth by Iain Morland and Annabelle Willox (2005) in their text *Queer Theory*: "What does it mean to describe oneself as queer? Is 'queer' an adjective, a noun or a verb? Is 'queer' something that you *do* or something that you *are?*" (p. 1). These questions lead to the two chief characteristics of queer theory that I will be considering in this discussion: the destabilization of the individual subject and the notion of identity as performative rather than constitutive (identity as practice). Having borrowed these perspectives, I may now consider their relevance to maternity. What are the possibilities that queer theory might offer to a completely radical revisioning of the concept of mother and the maternal subject?

Relevance of Queer Theory for Motherhood

At first glance, potential contradictions emerge in applying queer theory to a study of the maternal, especially in the case of mothers who are overwhelmingly presumed to be straight. Writing *In a Queer Time and Place*, Halberstam (2005) insists that

> queer uses of time and space develop, at least in part, in opposition to the institutions of the family, heterosexuality, and reproduction. They also develop according to other logics of location, movement and identification. If we try to think about queerness as an outcome of strange temporalities, imaginative life schedules, and eccentric economic practices, we detach queerness from sexual identity and come closer to understanding Foucault's comment in "Friendship as a Way of Life" that "homosexuality threatens people as a 'way of life' rather than as a way of having sex." (p. 1)

If queer time and space are viewed as explicitly opposite to family, heterosexuality, and reproduction, how can such concepts be fruitfully applied to mommybloggers, who most often identify as straight and who explicitly write about family and reproduction? Halberstam suggests, however, that the key attribute of queer time and space is their explicit disruption of the *institutions* of family, heterosexuality, and reproduction. In this respect, queer theory presents a useful method of interrogation for the mamasphere. Borrowing from Adrienne Rich's insight that the *institution* of motherhood oppresses, rather than the act of mothering itself, mommybloggers – even those who abide by the constraints of patriarchy quite consistently – can, in their examination of the challenges of motherhood, begin to question those constraints. In many cases, this is accomplished through a challenging of the shift towards unstable identity and subjectivity that occurs for many women as part of the transition to motherhood. Mommyblogger Elizabeth considers this shift in relation to parenting her four small children, writing on her profile page, "I am a mom . . . At some point in my life I had things that were interesting like a job and interests separate from kids. Maybe one day I can recapture my individuality."[5] While Elizabeth does not explicitly consider the possibility of a personhood between her individual self and the conjoined self she has become as a "mom," her blog shows a narrative of someone between self and mother. Her blog begins with her own voice and, interspersed with parenting tales, considers her own interests and ambitions by describing classes she takes and projects she accomplishes.

If Elizabeth is seen as a subject in transition, the door is opened to a transformation in the maternal subject from a fixed and inalterable role to a shifting and open-ended positionality. Many mommybloggers, like

Elizabeth, describe family, heterosexuality, and reproduction (to return to Halberstam's terms), yet do so in ways that challenge or at least
trouble in some way "natural" and reliable notions of these spaces.
Online mothers present "strange temporalities [and] imaginative life
schedules" (Halberstam, 2005, p. 1) – the outcomes of the complicated
and multiple lives that the range of people represented by the term
"mother" have to offer. For example, Elizabeth is a slightly different
mother to each of her children and her journey as mother is altered
throughout the course of her narrative. Furthermore, she articulates
the ways her identity will continue to shift away from motherhood
as primary focus towards a "recaptur[ing] of her individuality." It is
precisely the perceived impossibility of applying a queer response to
(often straight, or at least "straight") motherhood that makes this theoretical lens a requirement – the tacit acceptance of family, heterosexuality, and reproduction as stable terrain in contrast to queerness shows
the arena of motherhood as sorely lacking a liminal and contested critique, one which is best articulated by queer theorists.

If queer theory has been able to explode the categories of sexuality in
productive ways, and if Butler and other queer theorists have taken this
work into new realms in destabilizing the category of women, what
possibilities exist for motherhood studies in the unpacking of the category of mother? In order to best explore this notion, I will begin by considering some of the critiques often put forth towards a deconstructive
approach to identity categories.

Beginning in the 1990s, third wave feminists sought to acknowledge
and avoid the essentialism of earlier waves of feminism by moving towards a pluralist approach to feminism. As Jennifer Baumgardner and
Amy Richards (2000) wrote in the introduction to *Manifesta,* "We're not
doing feminism the same way that the seventies feminists did it; being
liberated doesn't mean copying what came before but finding one's
own way – a way that is genuine to one's own generation" (p. 130). At
the same time that queer theorists and third wave feminists were beginning to respond to concerns about essentialism, other feminist academics and activists were arguing that the destabilization of the subject
(female and/or gay or lesbian) was dismantling the political power of
these movements and, furthermore, was doing so just as women who
were historically on the margins were finally beginning to speak up.
Identity politics created communities, but these communities, born
of a desire for inclusion, were often characterized by dialogues about

exclusion. Queer theory emerged, in part, as a means to address these concerns.

Opponents argued that while hybrid and multivarious subjects allowed for an unprecedented range of perspectives, they would compromise the shared identities that engender activism and community-building. Halberstam (1991) argues against this point of view, suggesting that those who ask "why it is that subjecthood splinters when marginalized groups begin to speak" should note that

> the answer is already embedded in [the] question; subjecthood becomes problematic, fragmented, and stratified *because* marginalized Others begin to speak. The concept of the unified bourgeois subject, in other words, has been shot through with otherness and can find no way to regroup or re-unite the splinters of being. (p. 448)

Seen from Halberstam's point of view, the stable maternal subject emerges as mythical. While both diversity (the hybrid) and interpersonal relationality (the cyborg) may threaten the stable maternal subject, it is the performance of mothering itself that presents the greatest threat to motherhood as fixed terrain. By presenting a fundamental contextual interrelationship in the dependency of vulnerable children on their mothers, "mother" resists the notion of individual subjecthood in ways that draw fruitfully from queer theory's grappling with the same terrain. This conjoinment of mothers and their children and the repositioning of selfhood as a dyadic enterprise allows for a new understanding of both mothers and subjects more generally.

There is an incredible tension between the lived work that mothers – woman-identified parents – do and the need to de-gender the term to acknowledge the range of different possible social locations of mothers. On the one hand, it is politically necessary to speak of mothers. Attempts to de-gender terminology by speaking of "parenting labour" (without acknowledging that most of this labour is done by women – mothers) are disingenuous and are reminiscent of other realms of law and policy where feminist concerns have been de-gendered and have thus lost political relevance. On the other hand, while the word "mother" continues to come loaded with so many associations and expectations, it is a word that by necessity excludes the widest possible range of maternal experience. By considering that "mother," like "queer," is (hearkening back to Morland & Wilcox, 2005) "something you *do*," rather than "something you *are*," (p. 1) then we arrive at a reckoning that borrows the second major characteristic of queer theory: the understanding of identity as practice. Blended with the focus on incoherent subjectivity, such a reading of motherhood allows for the widest possible range of maternal beliefs and practices to exist harmoniously under the blanket term "mother." In a focus on both subjectivity and performativity, the mamasphere exemplifies motherhood as understood through a queer sensibility.

Illuminating the Queer Mother

If the word "queer" is predominantly defined by its opposition to normativity – its explicit nomenclature synonymous with "odd" or "peculiar" – can a similar alchemy be wrought with respect to the word "mother"? Is it possible to imagine a version of motherhood that presents a maternal subject *in opposition* to the institution of motherhood, to "mother against motherhood" (to borrow Rich's terminology) by defining "mother" as simply "not-from-motherhood"? If the queer subject, as positioned by queer theorists, is oppositional to the institution of homosexuality with its strict boundaries and expectations, what could a "not-mother," that is, a queer mother, bring to an analysis of motherhood? Such a shift would not simply be an act of semantic posturing; rather, by considering the ways that "queer" can inform "mother" in its role as a uniquely unstable descriptor, motherhood might well be shifted from a starkly defined enterprise to one more open to contradiction and ambiguity.

Arguably the queer mother has been struggling to emerge within feminist motherhood studies for some time in the troubling of individualist subjectivity (DiQuinzio, 1999; Chandler, 2007), a commitment to diversity, and a rejection of expert discourses (Nathanson & Tuley, 2008). Extending this understanding, the mamasphere provides a unique presentation of the queer mother. There is a correspondence between the two major traits of queer theory discussed above (the disruption of the individual subject and the emphasis on practice, rather than identity, as definitive) and two typical characteristics of mothering practice: the limits of individuality and performative conjoinment. In the context of the mamasphere, how do both this correspondence and the implications of queer motherhood for children in the realms of privacy and relationships shape mommyblogs? What is the role of individuality and performativity in shaping mothers?

Changing the Subject: Destabilizing Individuality

I gave birth to my son at a hospital. Months later, walking past the same building with my baby in his stroller, I was stunned at the fact that new life was materializing, moment by moment, in the building before me. How could it be that new humans were literally emerging constantly? What if the nurses were called upon to account for the number of patients? How could they meet this request when life was constantly splitting, one individual becoming two? When my daughter was born at home I was similarly bemused. I remarked to all who came to see her, "We were three. And now we are four. But *no one came into the house*."

The sanctity and individuality of human life are central to an antioppressive discourse in the West and are enshrined within the institution of motherhood. The health of a given constituency is measured by the life expectancy, education, and overall welfare of its *individual* citizens. Feminist thought equally entrenches individuality as a central theoretical premise. Patrice DiQuinzio (1999) suggests that

> feminism in the United States has to rely on individualism to claim women's equal human subjectivity, because the intelligibility and political effectiveness of this claim are a function of its being expressed in terms consistent with the dominant ideology. If feminism cannot show that women are subjects as individualism defines subjectivity, then it cannot argue for women's equal political agency and entitlement. (p. xiv)

DiQuinzio highlights a fundamental tension in contemporary feminist thought between seeing people as individual players in the context of law, policy, and citizenship, and, by contrast, seeing them as contextually defined. Certainly, within feminist theory and activism, the individuality of a child being strictly associated with its post-birth manifestation has been central to an acknowledgment of women's individual rights in the realm of abortion. Yet this carving of families into constituent parts ("we were one and now we are two") does not necessarily realistically represent the nature of mothering.

To consider mothers and children as distinct subjects implies that all subjects have rights and responsibilities. Children are immediately accorded rights by law (even though in practice many of these rights may be suspended for many children), but there is no discussion of how to manage responsibility in the presence of the total dependency of young life. Mothers have historically been expected to fill this gap with their caregiving labour, thus ensuring that as quickly as one splits into two, two immediately revert to one.

Rachel Cusk (2003) notes this tension in her memoir, *A Life's Work*, presenting a tacit view of a potentially queered motherhood:

> I read somewhere that it is inappropriate to refer to a mother and her new-born child as two separate beings: they are one, a composite creature best referred to as mother-baby or perhaps motherbaby. I find this claim un-nerving, even threatening, in spite of the fact that it perfectly describes the profound change in the co-ordinates of my being that I experience[d] in the days and weeks after my daughter's birth. I feel like a house to which an extension has been added: where once there was a wall, now there is a new room. I feel my heat and light flowing vertiginously into it. (pp. 93–4)

Mielle Chandler (2007) similarly suggests that "'mother' is an identity formed through a repetition of practices which constitute one as so pro-foundly interconnected that one is not one, *but is simultaneously more and less than one*" (p. 532).

While mothers and children are thus understood in the context of a discourse of individualism, their lived reality is one of conjoinment. While some popular parenting texts will celebrate this conjoinment as a symbiosis, a perfect union of mother and infant to the benefit of both, most mothers recognize that the utter dependency of one of the actors in this dyad instead renders the duality of mother and child parasitic rather than symbiotic. The infant child is granted a legal identity and a separate subjectivity, neither of which she initially re-quires; she does so at the expense of the mother's own subjectivity, a subjectivity that her mother may deeply crave. Furthermore, in en-trenching this relationality as natural, no further support from out-side the mother-child dyad is proffered for the mother who might herself require caregiving.

Shera, a mommyblogger and mother of six sons, experiences friction in responding to the contradiction between a cultural emphasis on in-dividuality and the tangible experience of relationality. She writes, "I struggle with our culture's need to focus solely on self and do whatever necessary to make self happy. So possibly in rebellion to that attitude I (and many other moms I know) buried myself in my family. No I don't feel that I lost my identity . . . it was altered yes, but lost . . . no."[6] Simi-larly, blogger Anne Nahm (a pun on "Anon") writes about her loss of self in new motherhood:

I let go of my job. I let go of the friends who didn't have kids and knew me as Anne. I traded in my Dry Clean Onlys for my Flowered Prints Hide Stains Best. If I had thirty dollars at a department store, the money went to a cute outfit for my child and not a cute shirt for me. I let go of the music I liked for Toddler Tunes. I let go of Spicy Thai Noodles and wine for Peanut Butter and Jelly sandwiches with carrot sticks. I talked with my husband about what our kids did that day, not what I did or thought. I surrounded myself with friends who talked about their kids and my kids and kids in general. I didn't know what any of my friend [Stay At Home Mom]s did prior to having kids. I read about kids and I talked about kids and I lived for my kids.

I don't regret most of it, because I did it for love. But it was foolish.[7]

In Anne's case, it is essential motherhood that leads to her loss of self. DiQuinzio (1999) skilfully dissects this tension in *The Impossibility of Motherhood: Feminism, Individualism and the Problem of Mothering*. She suggests that mothers are held to two contradictory expectations:

> Individualism and essential motherhood together position women in a very basic double bind: essential motherhood requires mothering of women, but it represents motherhood in a way that denies mothers' and women's individualist subjectivity. (p. xiii)

While DiQuinzio's analysis is sound, it is possible that even a non-essential motherhood cannot fully recognize the tangible needs required for the perpetuation of human life. How can mothers live an authentic, actualized existence while caregiving in the context of a society focused on individuated subjectivity? Shera and Anne grapple with this tension through blogging, negotiating the shift in identity that comes with parenting and the realization that their individual selfhood is necessarily constrained by their parenting labour. Writing with more frustration, the mother who blogs at *Mommy Sanctuary* wryly observes that "No one ever told me that when we stopped and revolved our lives around theirs that they would grow to believe that everyone revolves around them."[8] This blogger writes about her serious struggles with depression, but also reveals the challenge of living up to the societal expectation that mothers parent intensively (teaching children that a child-centred society is their due) while maintaining an individualized subjectivity for themselves. This contradiction is overwhelming.

There are two possible responses to this defilement of the cult of the individual and both responses are consistently given throughout the mamasphere. First, mothers may rail against the loss of their individual rights and direct that outrage towards the institution of patriarchal motherhood; this outrage is well expressed in the mamasphere. However, there is also another possible response found in mommyblogs: in exploring the spaces between individuals and in looking at the roles mothers play as "plural subjects" (Sommer, 1988), mommybloggers are quietly conceding that the focus on the individual has never truly carried over to women effectively. Annie, the mommyblogger behind *PhD in Parenting*, writes, "Almost all of us will take on a caregiving role at some point in our lives, whether we are caring for our children, our parents, our spouse or another friend or family member. We will all be involved in relationships with others that require us to sometimes consider the needs of others before our own."[9] Such an analysis of subjectivity shows the limitations and falsehoods perpetuated by a rigorous reckoning of individual subjecthood that hearkens back to the similar limitations put forth within a strict gender binarism; in this respect the lives of mothers thus present a threat that is similar (on a different axis) to that of the lives of queer subjects.

By acknowledging the very human reality of the dependency of the very young, we may begin to expose the notion of "both more and less than one" and replace it with a model that supports caregiving labour, adequately presenting – in policy and practice – the collective responsibility required to care for our collective vulnerability. "More and less than one" is thus transformed into, ideally, "many more than two." In the mamasphere, such a response can be seen in the emotional caregiving that mommybloggers provide for one another and the instrumental assistance born of the authenticity and dialogue therein. In the symbiosis between motherhood and blogging the incoherence of the mommyblog provides an interesting collective model that somehow pushes towards a notion of societies as collective organisms rather than masses of disparate individuals.

Mommybloggers are turning away from individualism, viewing its flaws and instead building an alternative model that focuses on breadth, diversity, collectivity, and relationality. They are presenting a version of subjectivity that allows for the same fluidity and porous boundaries allowed by a queer subjectivity. As Chandler (2007) writes, "The mistake lies not so much in equating motherhood with a loss of freedom and autonomy, but rather in adopting autonomy as an ideal"

(p. 536). Thus the mamasphere is an excellent hybrid of relational technology describing relational work – mothering and blogging in a wonderful symbiosis.

Such a symbiosis presents a queer mother in her rejection of the individual subject and her focus instead on the overlapping circles of community that define her, or any individual actor. To return to DiQuinzio, then, the relational mamasphere makes visible a queering of motherhood that responds to essential motherhood and makes an alternative reading possible. The key to the emergent queer-mother of the mamasphere, which exists in opposition to the institution of motherhood, can be seen in its major characteristics, already explicated in prior chapters. The hybridity of mommyblogs displays the diversity and breadth of maternal online writing; the mamasphere's cyborg relationality evidences the unique intersections and the collective autobiography that emerge from mommyblogs. At the nexus between these two traits is the queer mother presenting a subjectivity that is not easily contained, one that threatens the sanctity of the individual maternal subject.

How Mommyblogs Are Changing the Subject

While it is difficult to argue for the limits of individualism by providing examples of specific individual bloggers, it is nonetheless possible to examine the ways the mamasphere provides evidence of a literal "change of subject" towards a queer reckoning of motherhood. For example, in her essay "I Kid You Not: How the Internet Talked Me Out of Traditional Mommyhood," blogger Jennifer Gilbert (2009) provides an excellent example of a queering of maternal practice. Married at a young age, Gilbert took for granted that she would eventually become a mother. Upon reading and responding to mommyblogs, however, she found that she emphatically did not want to take on the realities that mommybloggers were describing. In describing her horror and relief at understanding the realities of motherhood before choosing to procreate, Gilbert quotes mommyblogger Heather of *Dooce*: "[If you] do not have kids and have wondered what life would be like, just go turn on a blender and stick your face in it. That." (quoted in Gilbert, 2009, p. 57). Gilbert's reactions to the real mothering work she saw online eventually culminated in her partner's vasectomy.

While Gilbert's piece is witty and charming, the real power in her essay comes from its conclusion, in which she eventually explores her discovery of nontraditional parenting blogs and makes the decision that she would like to become the foster mother of teenagers. Far from coming to this conclusion with the same dewy-eyed naïveté that characterized her earlier ideals about motherhood, Gilbert learned about the specific challenges that come with fostering older children through reading non-normative mommyblogs and concluded that these are the parenting burdens and difficulties that she is more interested in taking on. Her essay examines the specifics of individual subjectivity and the choice to welcome the interruption to this individualist ideology, but to do so in non-normative ways. Gilbert evidences a queer maternity in her capacity to broaden the possible paths to motherhood, but also in her view of herself as a subject who already lives within a pattern of relationships, including the blogging relationships that had a tangible effect on her personal path to maternity.

Deesha of *Mamalicious* presents a different response to the conjoinment of motherhood by chronicling an alternative template for the capacity for civil co-parenting with ex-partners. In Deesha's case, the mother-child dyad and the family nuclear triad are interrupted by alternative living arrangements. Divorced from her children's father, Deesha chooses to live apart from her present husband in order to maintain her co-parenting relationship with her ex-husband; her current husband, also civilly co-parenting, does the same in a different city. Deesha writes,

> Techboo and I get asked all the time, "How do you do it?" – "it" being maintain[ing] a long-distance relationship which will soon become a long-distance marriage . . . The short answer? He's got shared custody; I've got shared custody. Neither one of us wants to parent from a distance. So we do it because we love each other, love our kids, and are committed to being partners for life. The "how" flows from that: we make it work.[10]

Deesha presents a maternal subject ensconced within a web of potentially contradictory relationships; far from presenting an individual subject, she exemplifies queer motherhood by presenting the self-in-relation. She thus troubles existing notions of the stable maternal subject (as well as the institutions of both marriage and divorce), presenting instead both a strong individual voice and an unapologetic commitment to her communal existence.

On a more combative level, some mommybloggers have begun to expose the limits of individualism by engaging in online debates with nonmothers on the appropriate access of children to public spaces.

These debates take place in comments on mommyblogs and also in the writing of and commenting on childfree blogs, and often begin with childfree bloggers maligning mommybloggers for allowing their children to take up space – both literally and virtually, in the online realm. Anonymous blogger *Bitch Ph.D.* responds to the position that she and her son, referred to on her blog as "Pseudonymous Kid," should be less visible:

> [Children] are human beings. Actual members of society. Who, yes, happen to be in a dependent position. Nonetheless, inasmuch as they are members of society, they have a claim on society to help care for them in their dependence so that they do not starve. Now, since they have parents, there are many aspects of their dependence that society needn't bother with: y'all don't have to wipe Pseudonymous Kid's ass, you don't have to give him his bath, you don't have to read him mouse books over and over and over again . . .
>
> But yeah, goddamnit, you do have to deal with his presence in public spaces, even if he's acting like a little turd; you do have to recognize that because I have all that other stuff to do, I might be slightly less at the disposal of my employer for a few years (then again, no one should be at the disposal of their employer 24/7 anyway); you do need to deal with the times when I bring him into work because there is work I can't put off and there is no one else who can care for him on that day; and you do, I think, have an obligation to figure out social and economic policies that take into account the fact that this is not only my life, but the life of most adults at some point sooner or later.
>
> And in exchange, my friends, I and he have an obligation to deal with you when you have had a shitty day and are being a turd in a public space; or when you have to leave work early to pick up a friend at the airport or because you have opera tickets or a hot date; or when you have to call in sick; or when your illness turns out to be acute and far more expensive than any individual can afford; or when you get old and need to retire, and yadda yadda yadda.[11]

This post presents the essential characteristics of a revitalized queer mother-subject: an acknowledgment of the dyadic/conjoined nature of parenting practice, undertaken within the context of an open-ended and evolving medium. Such a method recalls Chandler's (2007) supposition that "recent developments in feminist queer theory . . . provide a nonessentialist framework for a deconstructive analysis of both the esteeming of the unencumbered separated subject and the devalued status of mothering" (p. 530).

These mommyblogs, then, indicate both the limits to individualism and the ways that a queer maternal subject can destabilize an individualist version of maternal subjectivity. This shifting subjectivity leads to the second key characteristic of a queer reckoning of motherhood: the foregrounding of the *act*, rather than the *identity*, of mothering.

From "Mother" to "Mothering"

If the consideration of the queer mother involves the discursive shift to an oppositional motherhood outside of the normative realm, then the second major effect of a queer reading of motherhood has similar linguistic implications in shifting "mother" from noun to verb. Specifically, a queer analysis of maternity allows for the possibility of motherhood as a lived practice rather than a fixed identity. Rich asks us, "What kind of beast would turn its life into words?/What atonement is this all about? – and yet, writing words like these, I'm also living" (quoted in Gilmore, 1994a, p. 66). The mamasphere allows for maternal subjects that are "also living" – women who inhabit real lives, with all their interruptions, contradictions, and complexities, presenting "mobile and transitory points of resistance" (Foucault, 1976, p. 96).

As discussed above, a move towards performativity is consistent with the terminological shift undertaken by many queer theorists towards considering queer identity as a descriptive and fluid marker rather than a structured and unyielding subjectivity. As Halberstam (2005) writes,

> ... not all gay, lesbian, and transgender people live their lives in radically different ways from their heterosexual counterparts, but part of what has made queerness compelling as a form of self-description in the past decade or so has to do with the way it has the potential to open up new life narratives and alternative relations to time and space. (pp. 1–2)

A similar shift exists within the realm of motherhood studies, beginning with Rich's (1976) insistence that "mothering" presented a much different view of maternal behaviour than "motherhood." Chandler (2007) argues that "'mother' is best understood as a verb, as something one does . . . " (p. 531). Borrowing from Butler's notion of performativity, Chandler goes on to suggest,

> To be a mother is to enact mothering. It is a multifaceted and everchanging yet painfully repetitive performance which although, like "woman," involves the way one walks, talks, postures, dresses and paints one's face, orients these activities directly and instrumentally in-relation to and with the walking, talking, posturing, dressing, undressing, dressing, undressing, dressing, undressing and painting of face (or, rather, the washing of paint off of face) of another who, due to a relation of near-complete interdependence, is not separate. (2007, p. 532)

While Chandler references motherhood as caregiving labour specifically, she nonetheless begins to consider mothers simply as those who mother, rather than ascribing an ossified and aggrandized view of the maternal subject. She writes, "No matter how hard one tries to 'hyperconform,' to simulate the perfect mother, the baby will always disrupt the simulation" (2007, p. 538). Chandler thus allows for a consideration of the ways that mothering, as a verb, begins to capture the true confusion and complexity of mothers' lives in a way that "Mother," as a noun, cannot.

Andrea O'Reilly (2008b) provides a more explicitly feminist take on the notion of motherhood as performative, suggesting that "feminist" models of maternity that focus exclusively on anti-sexist child-rearing neglect to consider the model that mothers present as they parent. Rather, through an analysis of her own mothering practices in dialogue with her two daughters, O'Reilly presents a view of feminist mothering as intrinsically performative, the act of an empowered mother who "shows" rather than "tells" her children how to respond to patriarchy.

The mamasphere is rich with examples of mothers who display a diversity of maternal practices and empowered subjectivities. The interruptions referenced by Chandler and the empowerment displayed by O'Reilly recur within the mamasphere, presenting a view of motherhood that is fundamentally queer in its insistence on mothering as descriptive rather than proscriptive.

Mommyblogger Deesha provides an example of the performative motherhood described by Chandler and O'Reilly. Writing again about co-parenting, Deesha asks,

> What does this look like in practice? We each do chores, grocery shopping, and cooking in both houses. We both stay up-to-date and as involved as we can be with all four girls' school and extracurricular activities. When

we are present or even long-distance, we've both helped with homework and school projects. TechBoo has scheduled Comcast and Dell service calls for me here. From my living room here, I've rescheduled dentist and doctors' appointments for him there.[12]

Deesha writes about the complicated mundanities of her day-to-day relationships – co-parenting her children with her ex-husband and helping to parent her step-children with her current husband. She does not simply provide overarching and generalized platitudes; by providing explicit details of her own life, Deesha shows the blogosphere an example of a non-normative parenting practice in action.

Blogger Alice of *Finslippy* unwittingly referencing one of O'Reilly's tenets of empowered mothering, suggests that the effect of such self-conscious sharing is access to authentic mothering experience:

> That's all we're after (I think) – some representation of authentic experience that we're not getting elsewhere. We sure as hell aren't getting it from the parenting magazines, which provide canned information about vaccinations and discipline and baking nutritious muffins that look like kitty cats, but will never help you feel less alone, less stupid, less ridiculous. This is the service we try to provide – we share our lopsided, slightly hysterical, often exaggerated but more or less authentic experiences. If one blogger writes about her traumatic doctor's visit, then maybe at some point, some freaked-out new mother is going to read that and feel a little better – less stupid, less ridiculous – about her own breakdown at the pediatrician's.[13]

By focusing on the practice of mothering rather than a falsified and limiting version of motherhood, Alice argues that blogs establish a mother's authenticity and create a community for her.

This focus on motherhood as personal practice rather than established discourse is made very explicit in the writing of one woman in particular, *Mamapundit* blogger Katie Allison Granju. In 1999, Granju wrote the book *Attachment Parenting: Instinctive Care for Your Baby and Young Child*. Extending the philosophies of Dr William Sears, Granju presented a very child-focused model of caregiving that, as I've written elsewhere (Friedman, 2008), can be viewed as anti-feminist. One of Granju's chief concerns in the text is to show that this particular parenting technique is not simply ideal but also biologically ordained. Indeed, the use of the word "instinctive" in the subtitle and the tone of the book suggest that mothers are naturally called to a child-centred model, and thus, that those who struggle with this model are either naturally defective or somehow insufficiently loving.

Granju's personal blog – in stark contrast to the wealth of her "expert" writing both on- and offline – presents a nuanced and personalized view of motherhood that offers great insight without falling in to the generalizing trap of expert discourse. Specifically, the great challenges she has faced in her life (notably, the tragic death of her teenage son Henry from a drug overdose in May 2010) point to a mother who is struggling with her mothering practice. Granju's blog presents a mother's critical uncertainty in practice, full of questions, grappling, ambivalence, and guilt; her expert writing presents a glib certainty embedded in a fixed maternal identity. Birthing her fifth child shortly after Henry's death, Granju writes the following blog entry about her struggles with breastfeeding:

> It's clear to me, a very experienced, knowledgeable breastfeeding mother with a high motivation to make nursing work, that this just wasn't going to happen for me this time. I know what it feels like when my body is producing milk, and I could tell almost immediately (although I tried to pretend it wasn't so in the first few weeks) that things were not working right this time around. There just wasn't any milk. I suspect that the biggest factor in my inability to produce milk at the moment is that my oldest child died in my arms only a few weeks before G was born. God only knows what the shock of that experience did to my body and its normal functioning.
>
> G is bottle fed. I am increasingly resigned to this, and I am trying to make peace with it, although it feels very weird.[14]

Granju's description of her life practice exposes a queer motherhood; that is, a motherhood that rests in the desperate compromises and imperfections of lived experience rather than in the idealized view of what mothers *ought* to accomplish. While Granju's experiences are obviously harrowing, one wonders whether her personal reckoning with breastfeeding might provide the kind of authentic comfort referenced by Alice above; that is, a release, for a new mother, from the potential desperation caused by the ceaseless celebration of breastfeeding in *Attachment Parenting*.

Granju, in her dual role as mommyblogger and parenting expert, made the difficult choice following the assault and overdose that led to her son's death to share his story publicly, revealing for the first time his addiction. Her choice opened her to fierce criticism that she was negating Henry's right to privacy, especially when he was initially thought to be likely to survive the experience. The concept of the queer mother as both performative and constitutive of a relational subjectivity has specific implications for children whose own subjectivities are implicated in both the notion of a conjoined subjecthood and a descriptive view of mothering practice shared online. In order to truly consider the queer mother, then, it is necessary to look more closely at "queering the children," which involve issues of subjectivity and privacy.

Queering the Kids: Mommyblogging and Privacy

Blogger Maria of *Mommy Melee* insists that "This is my story – the way I choose to tell it and when I choose to tell it . . . I decide what to share about my children, about my spouse, about the people around me who shape my days and shape who I am."[15] Maria is to be applauded for her conviction and her insistence on owning her own story; but what about the implications of her blogging practice for the people whose stories she reveals?

If a queer view of motherhood allows for a relational subjectivity, a dyadic identity model, then what becomes of the arguably vulnerable subjects who are displayed alongside (and by) their mothers? If a queer motherhood is performative, what are the implications for the supporting cast and what, specifically, becomes of individual children's right to privacy? What are the effects of mommyblogging on children as they grow up? It is these questions to which I now turn, considering the ways that a shifting queer maternity may provide a new way of reading the privacy debate within the mamasphere.

Since the inception of the mamasphere, mommybloggers have been accused of abusing the privacy of the children they include in their writings. Initially, this may have been due to the whole notion of blogging as a suspect and overly revealing practice. As mommyblogger Alexa writes,

Five years ago, when I told people I wrote about my personal life on the Internet, they looked at me as if I'd just said I spent my free time masturbating in public parks. "*Why?*" they'd ask, disgusted. "Why would you want to do such a thing?" Now they just nod, like: *Of course you do.* Now they ask me how much money . . . I make doing it, this writing online, this blogging, and when I tell them I don't make much of anything they revert back to their suspicious "Why?"-ing of yesteryear.[16]

Even as blogging has come to be accepted as a practice, mommybloggers continue to be held to a higher standard than other bloggers. It has become a criticism so common it is almost trite, the concern that little Billy will grow up and google himself to find both the most embarrassing moments of his childhood revealed, and (more traumatically?) the depths of his mother's ambivalence exposed. Yet the specific ideologies presented within this critique originate in idealized and patriarchal versions of motherhood that are deeply embedded in notions of "good" motherhood.

Mommybloggers are themselves keenly self-conscious of the issue of both personal privacy and the privacy of their children. According to *Finslippy's* Alice[17] in her survey of many popular mommybloggers, the consensus is that "above all . . . we have a responsibility to protect our children."[18] Despite frequent discussion and care taken to protect children from scrutiny, however, mommybloggers are consistently perceived as exploitative and foolhardy.

Blogger Marie notes, "As both Bryan and Caitlin get older, I try to hold back on the writing and keep their lives private. Plus, if they ever decided to write a blog, yikes, the 'Mom' stories they could pay me back with! J/K . . . sorta."[19] Despite her concerns, Marie continues to update her blog with information, carefully selected, about her grown children. In continuing to write about them, Marie acknowledges that her children's lives are still occurring within the context of her own. In doing so, she blends her concerns about her children's privacy with an acknowledgment of their conjoined subjectivity.

Given that mommybloggers seem to negotiate the issue of privacy for children fiercely and constantly, it is remarkable that outsiders – other types of bloggers and journalists, most notably – are quick to seize on an un-nuanced reckoning of privacy concerns as a means of diminishing maternal writing. Ayelet Waldman, blogger and author of a number of books including *Bad Mother* (2009), used her blog as a means of exposing her declining mental health. When Waldman, who suffers from depression, referred to her blogging practice as a lifeline on National Public Radio (in the United States), she was excoriated for revealing, *as a mother,* her authentic self. Commentator Jessica G. from the online magazine *Jezebel* suggested,

It's wonderful that Waldman got the help she needed, and of course, destigmatizing mental illness is incredibly important. But I can't imagine what it would feel like to be her child and read, in real time, about how my mother was trying to kill herself.[20]

In response, *MamaPop* contributor Jane asks,

Most bloggers and other memoirists take very seriously the issue of how their stories might be received – in the moment or in the future – by their families. But here's my quibble, and it's a big, angry quibble: those bloggers and memoirists and writers aren't just *mothers*. Why single out *mothers*?

The . . . primary question – "when does airing familial dirty laundry cross the line between art and mass destruction?" – is one that can and should be asked of memoirists in general. But that would include, I presume, Augusten Burroughs, and not just his mother. We might also ask it of David Sedaris, or, reaching further back, of Boswell or Rousseau or Libanius. The genres of memoir and autobiography have been dominated by men for millenia [*sic*]: why single out women for finally lifting the veil on their worlds – worlds that have long been expected to be kept shuttered and private and hence excluded from public discourse – and then shit on them for it?[21]

Jane's comments are a reminder that there are many sites of life writing and that mothers are uniquely castigated in them; in other words, mommybloggers are exploiting their children because they are mothers, not because they are blogging. The dominant discourse of patriarchal motherhood is thus exposed, revealing the unsubtle view that mothers ought to subsume their own positionality – to a greater extent than any others – in order to protect their children. In this critique, the ridiculousness of individualist discourse is further revealed: in the case of small children, mothers are the keepers of their stories, but are meant to subsume their own shared tales in order to ensure that they protect their children from scrutiny or future embarrassment. Furthermore, this need is presented as binary – bad mothers write about their children online, while good mothers do not – ignoring the fact that many mommybloggers are constantly attempting to balance the needs of their children with their own needs for authenticity and community.

These concerns are not new to mothers and extend beyond life writing to other media. In her book *Family Frames*, Marianne Hirsch

(1997) describes the experiences of artist Sally Mann, who, after a brilliantly successful show of her photographs of her children, faced harsh criticism:

> The three hundred pictures Mann so successfully sold are all photographs of her three children . . . many of them nude shots taken during the four to five years preceding their adolescence. The "six to nine months" she spent in the darkroom "to fill orders," the critics imply, are months she presumably did not spend caring for her children, but instead remaking them into flat surfaces, reinventing them for public consumption, in a time frame which, ironically, approximates gestation. (p. 151)

Here Hirsch explores many of the themes that trouble critics of mommyblogs: that children are exploited, that they become the products of their parents' writing, and that, tacitly, mothers ought to be doing more mothering and less writing about their lives and the lives of and their children. Hirsch goes on, however, to suggest that mothers who reveal their children to the public are, simultaneously, revealing themselves, suggesting that only in acknowledging the presence of "motherbaby" can we grant permission for mothers to create and document their own lived experiences with their children.

Author Rachel Pastan gives another example of the challenge of privacy for mothers in offline sites such as fiction. In an article on *Babble.com* discussing her novel *Lady of the Snakes*, Pastan describes her careful effort to create a description of a baby that was as different as possible from her own child in order to avoid the potential for limiting her daughter's privacy. Yet she comes to a conclusion that is very similar to Hirsch's understanding. Many years after writing her novel, when her 13-year-old daughter read the book, the teen's concern is not with the child described therein, but with the mother.

> "These feelings Jane has about Maisie," she asked, "were they your feelings?"
>
> My instinct was to lie to her. But she's too old to lie to, and besides, one day she may have children of her own.
>
> "Yes," I said, and we waited together in the sunny living room while she took that in.
>
> Not, *Is that baby me?* but *Is that mother you?* I saw then, for the first time, that they were the same question. If the mother was me, then the

baby was her by definition. How laughable my efforts to keep the real and
fictional babies separate![22]

Pastan reveals the inability to adequately separate mother and child –
in art, as in life – as well as her own honest attempt to protect her child.
As Mir, author of the blog *Woulda Coulda Shoulda*, remarks, "Sometimes what happens here has to stay in the cone of silence, because I
feel strongly that sharing would be painful for the kids, down the road.
(I'm fresh out of crystal balls, too, so I'm always guessing. Always. And
this is why God invented guilt, and therapy)."[23] Mir's remarks suggest
that mommyblogging, like all other aspects of mothering, is an imperfect and challenging work in progress, one that may potentially harm
children in the future but may also do great good for both children and
mothers. In other words, it is no more intrinsically harmful than any
other aspect of parenting practice, and mothers who blog overwhelmingly do their best, and hope for the best, exactly as they do in other aspects of their parenting and their own lives.

Concerns over the negative capacity of mommyblogging seem to
recall the apocryphal "Mommy Wars" wherein working mothers and
stay-at-home mothers were seen as endlessly in conflict. In reality,
these alleged "wars" were largely created by media *about* (rather than
by) mothers. Similarly, criticisms of mommyblogs are largely put forth
by those outside the mamasphere and seem to focus on a tacit critique
of mothers daring to do something for themselves rather than subsuming themselves completely to their children.

Notably, if mommyblogging were really so critically dangerous to
children, one would expect that the children of the earliest mommybloggers (who are now reaching adolescence for the most part) would
have begun to use the Internet as a means of speaking back to their exploitative and horrific mothers. Yet approximately a decade after the
birth of the mamasphere there is no evidence of any such critique. In
reifying dominant discourses of motherhood, the privacy critique of
mommyblogging suggests that the mamasphere highlights a queer
motherhood that exists as a threat in its focus on a motherhood that is,
to use Elspeth Probyn's (1996) term, "outside belonging":

As a theoretical term and as a lived reality, I pose the term *outside belonging* against certain categorical tendencies and the rush to place difference
as absolute . . . in the face of the fixity of the categorical logic of identity,

I seek to instill some of the movement that the wish to belong carries, to consider more closely the movement of and between categories. (p. 9)

If mommyblogging allows for a motherhood outside belonging, what are the possibilities that such a motherhood might allow for children beyond a hackneyed concern about their roles as potential victims? Perhaps a queer motherhood that considered the limits of the individual subject could acknowledge the deep challenge not of mommyblogging but of mothering: mothers *do* control their children's autonomy and indeed are entirely expected to do so; mothering rests only uneasily within/alongside individualism. The foregrounding of such a view within the mamasphere provides tantalizing potential for children.

Children of mommybloggers may be less likely to be hampered by the digital divide; such children themselves are growing up with technology, and thus connectivity, central to their development. As a result, children of mommybloggers may begin to access a queer politic that emphasizes connection. As children grow in the context of the expanding matrix of the web, their notions of privacy and individuality might be quite different from those of their parents' generation. Instead of assuming that their identities are kept private, children are becoming aware that they are exposed – sometimes by their mothers, but increasingly by themselves. As a result, their expectations may have shifted from those of previous generations. Many mommybloggers are fierce about their children's privacy and eliminate their children's stories from blogs as these children grow up. Others, however, are able to include their children in their blogs as a shared project. This is the case for Georgia of *I Am Bossy*, who has included a new feature on her popular blog titled "Notes From A Far-Flung Correspondent." This feature includes occasional posts written by her college-aged son about his life, friends, and community. Importantly, these posts are geared towards *I Am Bossy*'s audience and thus differ significantly from what Georgia's son might write on a blog of his own, though it appears that his posts are entirely of his own creation and not, for example, edited by Georgia to suit her site. Georgia's unnamed son has become part of the fabric of the blog, using his own voice to contribute to this collective project. Likewise, Georgia's teenaged daughter is occasionally featured in posts, presumably with her consent.

The arena for questioning thus shifts from issues of privacy to the level of comfort with which "millennial generation" children will perceive their parents' writings. Blogger Grace from *State of Grace* discusses the way she negotiates her writing with her children comically: "I blogged about the time Molly threw a party at the house without my permission and part of her punishment was that I got to blog about it."[24] Grace's comment suggests that her daughter generally gets to control access to her own stories appearing on her mother's blog and that the punishment was thus an aberration. For Molly (and teenagers like her), there is an awareness of her mother's power in documenting their shared story, but also the controls placed on that power.

Access to mommyblogs will allow children to view their own childhoods as intensely complicated and codependent pursuits: they will see their mothers in communities, but will also see themselves as intimately connected to their parents in their own infancies and early childhoods. Thus it may happen that future netizens are much more at ease with the context of the blogosphere and its relationality. Indeed, while this immersive connective experience is much decried as a sign of the fall of civilization, it is possible to surmise that young people, and the children who are quickly following them, will understand the value of webs of connections as intensely relevant to a sense of self – surrounded by constant contact, such young people may begin to undermine the individualistic self, text by text.

Perhaps the most important implication of mommyblogs for young people comes not in stories about themselves in isolation but in the mamasphere's ability to tell stories about mothers and mothering. As discussed earlier, Western society tends to reduce maternal identity to a set of immutable and unattainable characteristics. Children are silent witnesses to their own parenting, unable to recall the nuances of their own infancy and early childhood. Indeed, it is arguable that children can only remember their parenting as it becomes combative. By reading not only about their mothers' struggles, but also about their mothers' obvious love and care, perhaps adult children may find their relationships with their mothers bolstered rather than damaged. Whether the outcomes are positive or negative, mommyblogs allow children to see their mothers as three-dimensional individuals, to combat the sense of "just *my* mom" with "just *a* mom." Mothers are portrayed in the mamasphere as complex and contradictory individuals, and mother-love becomes visible as both intense and contested.

In earlier chapters I referred to Heather Armstrong's blog *Dooce*, in which she recorded her depression. Many readers of *Dooce* have wondered about the implications of her harrowing stories of postpartum depression for her daughters as they grow up. While it is certainly possible that Heather's daughters, as adolescents, will use her exhaustive archive as evidence of her "poor" parenting, it is arguable that were the archive erased, they would easily find some other evidence of her purported shortcomings. In the pre-Internet era, adolescents had no shortage of sites of conflict with their parents and relied on nondigital resources for their complaints. Of more interest, however, is the effect that this archive might have on Heather's children – and all the children of mommybloggers – as they approach parenthood themselves. In reading about their mother's struggles, Leta and Marlo may see a raw and unvarnished picture of an alternative motherhood, a queer motherhood. Instead of the rosy glow of hindsight, these young women will be able to access their own mother's voice as she navigated this intensely challenging terrain – and this, in turn, may support them in their own parenting journeys. Writing directly to her daughters, Heather asks,

> Will you resent me for this website? Absolutely. And I have spent hours and days and months of my life considering this, weighing your resentment against the good that can come from being open and honest about what it's like to be your mother, the good for you, the good for me, and the good for other women who read what I write here and walk away feeling less alone.
>
> And I have every reason to believe that one day you will look at the thousands of pages I have written about my love for you, the thousands of pages other women have written about their own children, and you're going to be so proud that we were brave enough to do this.
>
> We are an army of educated mothers who have finally stood up and said pay attention, this is important work, this is hard, frustrating work and we're not going to sit around on our hands waiting for permission to do so. We have declared that our voices matter.[25]

Jennifer Sinor's (2002) wonderful book *The Extraordinary Work of Ordinary Writing* pulls together the diaries of her great-great-great aunt, Annie Ray. In considering her motivation for creating such a text, Sinor writes about her own reflections on her childhood:

> It began with the realization that as a family we had consumed almost everything ever created by my mother. The imprint of my fathers' hand remains publicly held in the treaties and negotiations found in military law

books. Look into any military document on matters of international ocean law in the Persian Gulf in the 1980s and my father appears. However, we have eaten all that my mother has made, worn through the couches she has recovered, outgrown all the clothes she has sewn. To measure her worth by her record, by what remains recorded, renders her almost invisible. (p. 2)

Mommyblogging, for an unprecedented range of women, reverses that invisibility, constructing windows through which they can see and be seen. Perhaps the most potent and valuable implication of the mamasphere for children, then, is its value as an archive challenging the silence of motherhood – imperfectly and incompletely, but nonetheless giving tomorrow's mothers and fathers a view behind the rose-coloured lenses of their own imperfectly recalled childhoods. As Alice of *Finslippy* suggests,

It's a tricky dance to execute, but the concerns about embarrassing your kids are often outweighed by the rewards they might reap from your writing. There are amazing moments I have tried to capture, that otherwise would be lost forever. And if I share the times when I'd like to leave him outside with a packed suitcase and a sign that says "free boy," I really believe that acknowledging those feelings is going to benefit him in the long run.[26]

Making the Queer Shift

A queer view of mommyblogs presents potentially surprising congruities between maternity and queer subjectivity. In focusing on both the limitations of the project of subjecthood and the need to replace stable subjects with performative approaches to identity, both queer and mommyblogging subjects thus allow for a view of the self that is porous and interruptable, a working knowledge that exists against understanding and definition. Mommyblogs threaten our understanding of individuated selfhood and, as a result, portray some of the same range of possibilities that queer theory's similar threat achieves.

There is fear associated with this shift: if we don't understand, in a coherent way, who mothers *are*, how can we acknowledge the ways that motherhood is hard? How can we respond to patriarchy and other oppressive conditions that make motherhood even harder? Can we gather, as a community of mothers, to make mothers' lives better? Fundamentally, however, motherhood has never been a coherent enterprise, and an acknowledgment in the life writing of mommy-bloggers of both the performative and contextual nature of maternity may be required in order for a continued fruitful study of maternity. DiQuinzio (1999) acknowledges the trepidation with which motherhood activists and scholars may approach this shift, yet argues that it is inevitable:

> Feminist theory will have to focus on specific instances of mothering in specific contexts in order to analyze in detail the complex processes of over-determination that differently constitute mothering in different material, social, and ideological contexts. Feminist theory will also have to theorize the ways in which the subject position "mother" is variously and contradictorily constituted, so that the experience of being a mother is more or less partial, divided, fragmented, and even incoherent. Perhaps most importantly, feminist theory will have to be critically vigilant about its conflicted relationship to individualism and about its own desires for the experience of the complete and coherent subjectivity that individualism promises but never provides. (p. 244)

Mommyblogs present one possible space in which to meet DiQuinzio's challenge. Mommyblogs allow for a shift from a coherent and stable isolated maternal subject to one that moves from the centre towards the contextual margins: a queer motherhood defined by the *absence* of normativity rather than the *presence* of any singular coherent characteristic, by the collective mothering of many actors alongside their children, rather than an apocryphal and petrified motherhood. Such a motherhood presents the only kind of mothering community that is truly inclusive and responsive and hearkens instead to the alternatives put forth by Iris Marion Young. Young (1990), rejecting traditional communities, argues,

> The ideal of community presumes subjects can understand one another as they understand themselves. It thus denies the difference between subjects. The desire for community relies on the same desire for social wholeness and identification that underlies racism and ethnic chauvinism on the one hand and political sectarianism on the other. (p. 302)

Young suggests that we reject communities in favour of "unoppressive cities" that describe not a physical space but "a *kind of relationship* of people to one another, to their own history and one another's history" (1990, p. 318). Such a mythical "unoppressive city" sounds like the place in which the queer mother may reside, a virtual location that may already exist within the vast terrain of the mamasphere.

6   Conclusion

Ah, blogging. you make everything just a little less lonely, at least.
— Bon, *Crib Chronicles*[1]

As I was reading through mommyblogs in researching this book, I was unable to scroll through my list of selected blogs in a linear fashion. As I pored over any given blog, I was drawn to comments, and would click to a commenter's blog to finish the discussion, retreat to a mommyblogger's archive to gain context, or pause and google an external reference. I found "hypertext" to be aptly named as it effectively disrupted the stable, staid, and idealized research process (much like mommyblogs disrupt notions of motherhood). I was hyperactively hopping around, gathering information in a peripatetic fashion. As blogger Antique Mommy writes,

> I think the single most thing I love about blogging is its serendipitous nature. Oft times I'll click on a link on a blogroll and then another and another and like a beagle, I'll end up somewhere far from where I started and have no idea how I got there. Using that approach to the Internet and life, I've met a lot of nice people, made some new friends and discovered some really incredible writers.[2]

On the one hand, this method of research was undoubtedly frustrating; on the other hand, this method of reading impressed upon me the ways that "mommies" who blog are producing such a wide range of writing about their lives, a kaleidoscope of intellectual thought and insights, opinions and analyses, conversation and support. Mommybloggers are reflecting the multifaceted practice of mothering as a diverse population of literate women going public with their hybrid and cyborg lives.

In reading these mommyblogs, I noticed the confusion and slipperiness of mothering *in the world*; the imperfections and contradictions as well as the intersections between infinite points of social location that work upon any given mother to participate in her mothering practice. The stability of the term "mother" has been exploded and in its place a contested subject – a queer subject – has emerged, one that represents this churning, inconsistent, and constantly evolving experience. It is a mother in flux that offers real and important possibilities for those who are eagerly consuming this knowledge and searching for a more politicized understanding of subjecthood.

To appreciate just how much mommyblogs offer in this pursuit, they need to be read as an endless and practically infinite conversation with millions of participants, full of confusion and aberration. Furthermore, the lack of temporality of the mamasphere (and, more generally, the blogosphere) means that as I sit writing this book, the conversation in the mamasphere is continuing, and by the time I click over "there" the next discursive event will have already occurred and still more will be unfolding. In this process, blogging (and especially mommyblogging in its focus on the nexus of personal and political) departs completely from traditional individualistic notions of subjectivity with the presumption of a stable individual author. Instead, mommybloggers are collectively creating a dynamic cyberorganism that is endlessly evolving.

Given the evolving nature of mommyblogs and the conversation they engage in, is it possible to draw firm conclusions? Indeed, the writings are deeply reflective of contemporary motherhood and of the "ambivalence, confusion, and turbulence that may characterize its practices" (Kinser, 2008, p. 123). But does this turbulence shift the meaning of motherhood?

The mamasphere may resist what Judith Baxter (2008) perceives as the explicit "healing agenda" of much analytical work and may allow instead for a "transformative quest" that maintains an openness to instability and ambiguity (p. 246). In order to consider this quest, it is necessary first to look towards possible future directions for this medium.

Precariousness of the Medium

Barbara Johnson suggests that "to judge from recent trends in scholarly as well as popular literature, three crucial questions can be seen to stand at the forefront of today's preoccupations: the question of mothering, the question of the woman writer, and the question of autobiography" (quoted in Gudmundsdóttir, 2003, p. 97). The mamasphere may indicate the culmination of these preoccupations in a uniquely self-referential and interactive medium. Given the mamasphere's potential as a record of a shifting maternal sensibility, it is important to consider the potential precariousness of these archives.

In the months between selecting blogs for this study and reading blogs, some were taken down, while others became password protected or only allowed access to select components of their archive. The Internet exists as an unprecedentedly extensive repository, but ultimately online content can be extremely ephemeral. As discussed with respect to temporality, online authors, while obviously constrained by dominant discourses, are free not only to write their stories in their own voices but also to change, remove, or limit access to those stories. By contrast, authors of more traditional media such as books and magazines effectively allow the public to own a copy of such media *ad infinitum*. The books on my shelf are mine and, barring fire or flood, remain mine whether the publisher declares bankruptcy, the author reneges, or the story evolves. Unless I save blog posts onto my own computer, however, they are only available to me for as long as their authors allow access and as long as technology continues to evolve in modes that allow access to earlier iterations of blogs.

This lack of permanence contributes to the precariousness of the medium but also to the empowerment of the author. There is room in an online narrative to return to earlier writing with a link or a footnote heralding changed opinions, and there is always the option of outright removal. While removed text will linger in Google's cache for some time, it will nonetheless become unavailable to the general public in moments. This precariousness is notable especially with regard to concerns about children's privacy. While I am hopeful that future children will let the new picture of motherhood that is now emerging in the blogosphere help them understand their mothers as subjects-in-relation, if such children reading their parents' archives are instead, in some cases, shamed or traumatized by stories of their childhoods, the option exists to protect or remove these stories at a keystroke. While such control ultimately rests in the hands of the author of any given blog – that is, a mother rather than her children – it does *not* rest with every individual who has ever read the blog. This is in stark contrast to other media (such as motherhood memoirs), which allow for much more straightforward and consistent access to the writing by non-authors.

A different kind of precariousness exists in the mamasphere and, indeed, across the blogosphere as a whole: the precariousness born of sheer abundance. As the mamasphere proliferates astronomically, the capacity to accurately access material may become increasingly difficult; even the most sophisticated search engines are largely inefficient in the face of such a wealth of material. Furthermore, this challenge may be more acute within the mamasphere where the particularities that set mommyblogs apart from one another tend not to rest in great events but instead in personal details. It will be interesting to note whether Internet users collectively create a cataloguing system that begins to more successfully mine the mountain of online content into more discernible categories; it will be even more interesting to consider how mommyblogs may be further ghettoized or marginalized in the context of such categorization.

Alternate/Alternative Technologies

While millions of mommyblogs exist, many new mothers in the last two or three years have turned to Facebook as a way to archive their private stories and share information about their families. While an analysis of the maternal content on Facebook is a project in and of itself, it is important to at least consider the ways that this medium tends to present a more uniform experience, both visually and textually. By providing finite methods of interaction, Facebook flattens some of the unique opportunities provided by blogging software. Facebook would seem to privilege the relational but ultimately does so by entrenching individuals as singular users. A cursory examination of Facebook use by mommybloggers suggests that Facebook engenders less critical and shorter posts. This is emphatically not the case with another major emergent social media platform, Twitter. In stark contrast to Facebook, Twitter seems to augment, rather than supplant, many mothers' blogs. Furthermore, the application has been used as a source of activism, with its real-time methodology and easy and quick readability creating fascinating (and sometimes terrifying) social movements. In particular, Twitter changes the whole face of mommyblogging by circumventing the capacity of bloggers to close comments: if any of *Dooce*'s million Twitter followers object to one of her blog posts they can tweet their disapproval, whether comments are open or closed. While Twitter is, again, beyond the scope of this project, future analysis of the mamasphere will need to consider the ways that these new applications will change and are already changing online maternal life writing.

Monetization and a Changing Voice

The concerns presented above presuppose that mothers will choose to continue to document maternal experiences in some of the same ways that they have in the past. Such suppositions may not be supported by an examination of emergent trends in the mamasphere. Mommyblogs are becoming increasingly monetized and are thus changing in content. Whether mommybloggers should or should not monetize is not under discussion; rather, the question is whether the current mamasphere will be recognizable as such trends in marketing continue. Will a consideration of the implications of maternal life writing be irrelevant in five or ten years, as "mommyblogs" come more to describe a particular marketing tool largely devoid of personal content? And, if so, will a different genre emerge for women who continue to want to use the Internet as a repository for personal content? Monetization is changing the style of "women's writing": instead of the traditional (and arguably stereotypical) style that foregrounds intimate and personal knowledge, writers – women – are supplanting personal content with content calculated to generate revenue or free products from sponsors.

While discussion of the ethics and practices of blogging for money (albeit, in most cases, negligible sums) has affected the entire blogosphere, mommybloggers seem to be especially scrutinized. Perhaps due to their mining of personal anecdotes or the perceived vulnerability of the children about whom they blog, mommybloggers have been held to a higher standard with respect to monetization. Among mommybloggers, there is some fear that monetization will result in a less sincere and raw documentation of motherhood in the trenches. Others argue that women who write will deserve the recognition and monetary compensation that any good writer should see. This schism is ongoing within the mamasphere and will undoubtedly continue to provide fodder for endless debate in years to come.

The debate exposes the key concern, which is not that blogs should never display ads, feature giveaways, or increase their monetization, but that many mommybloggers are no longer blogging about their experiences of motherhood. Instead, they are reviewing products *for* mothers, providing advice *for* mothers. In other words, these bloggers are marketing *to* women, without the platform of their own honest experiences as a background to the products under review. Some mommybloggers fear that the narrative and diaristic component of mommyblogs – the very aspects that initially led to scorn and derision, but that are considered by some inside the community as the hallmarks of the mamasphere at its best – are under attack. Jenn of *Mommy Needs Coffee* writes,

In the past year or so a new crop of mommybloggers has popped up. Many women who are a part of this new breed of mommybloggers have come to the scene heralding with much pomp and circumstance a sense of entitlement. They feel they are owed something. They feel just by slapping the label mommyblogger on their blog (blogs where they barely if ever write about their personally [sic] lives or families at all), they have earned the same respect as those who are writing quality stories that engage their readers.[3]

Jen's concern hinges on the need for mommybloggers to write about their "personal lives or families" in order to maintain both the authenticity and intimacy that the mamasphere requires. Not all mommybloggers agree. Popular mommyblogger Amalah writes,

six short years on the Web and I'm a freaking dinosaur, apparently, but I guess my point is that there has always been something threatening the community. We have been on the brink of sellout-y destruction for as long as I've been doing this, and I'm pretty sure me and my weirdly-named blog and TWOP-aping writing style were once considered harbingers of literary doom and made fun of on some old-skool message board. Now we all just get to overreact on Twitter.[4]

The mamasphere allows mothers to explore the intimacy of women who write about their children and families and consider the implications of these narratives and, most importantly, the connections between their authors within the constellation of connectivity provided by the World Wide Web. This connection is, in the end analysis, typified in the debate, contradiction, and ongoing documented discussion of monetization. The cyborg nature of the connected mamasphere provides an astronomical range of divergent points of view in dialogue with one another.

Monetized mommyblogs have the same range of quality as any other mommyblogs; some accomplish monetization skilfully while others falter. For example, in September 2007 mommyblogger Kellie wrote a post responding to the question, floating from blog to blog at that time, "Does your blog have a purpose?":

Personally, I don't know that I blog for a purpose other than personal satisfaction. A gratifying moment for me and my blog is when someone leaves a sweet comment in response to what I have posted. I get just a touch of this "I've arrived" feeling, even though that is so far from the truth. I blog because I enjoy sharing my feelings.[5]

Three days later, Kellie posted the following:

Do you own any Bush furniture? If you don't and you're unsure as to what exactly Bush furniture is, keep reading! Bush furniture is a manufacturing company that has been making great quality furniture for a long time! Their products are so unique and "clean" looking that I've even considered buying some myself. If you're looking for new home or office furniture, consider Bush furniture. Quality furniture at a competitive price![6]

Subsequent posts from Kellie contained further blatant product placement; the personal content on her blog dwindled and was then eliminated almost entirely. Kellie may have monetized successfully, yet there is no question that her voice changed completely as a result of her choice to monetize. While other mommybloggers may synthesize sponsored content more skilfully, the question of whether product placement shifts the maternal voice remains cogent.

Monetization and diversity

It is significant that the products generally selected for either advertisement or giveaways entrench patriarchal motherhood by reminding mothers that their role is to clean, cook, and care for children almost exclusively; monetization also assumes a level of class privilege in the inclusion of advertisements for furniture and resorts that, ironically, many of the mothers who are monetizing their blogs may not have. Finally, monetized mommyblogs may further entrench the relationship between the institution of motherhood and rampant consumerism by making explicit the notion that, in order to mother well, one must purchase endlessly. Ironically, however, many of the unknown mothers who monetize may do so precisely because they cannot afford the "necessities" required for good motherhood. Furthermore, while the mamasphere may be diverse (though clearly not representatively so), monetized mommyblogs are not. Marketing companies have specifically sought out mommybloggers who conform to the mythical norm of middle-class, heterosexual, married, and white motherhood. This was notably discussed at BlogHer 2007 when Stefania Pomponi Butler pointed out the number of approaches her blog *City Mama* had received from a variety of marketing sites. Her second blog, *Kimchi Mamas*, focused on Korean culture and identity, had not been approached once. Addressing her question to a public relations executive, Butler asked why mothers of colour were being ignored within the quest to monetize:

> He admitted, "You're right. We don't pitch to bloggers of color." And here's the money quote: "*We just don't know what to do with them.*"
> Yes, I did thank him for making me feel like a second class citizen.[7]

Following this exchange, many corners of the mamasphere briefly lit up with discussions of race, status, and identity. By BlogHer 2008, a specific session on pitching to mommybloggers of colour was incorporated into the conference schedule. Ironically, however, these discussions and "solutions" served only to highlight the extent to which the mamasphere is still completely presumed to be populated only by white, middle-class mothers; a presumption that pervades the institution of motherhood itself. By assuming that mothers are white and that black mothers, for example, require a qualifying adjective, dominant discourses of motherhood are exposed as racist. Perhaps even more disturbingly, the perceived racelessness of white mothers is likewise unacknowledged, leaving race and racism as topics of discussion relevant only to nonwhite mothers and bloggers. As monetization pervades the mamasphere, the influence of marketing on content may erode the potential for the mamasphere to act as a heteroglossia, a space for a multitude of diverse viewpoints. Rather, the twin influences of monetization and patriarchal motherhood may serve to entrench the tacit assumption of mothers as white, able, and straight. Mothers of children with disabilities, trans-mothers, non-English-speaking mothers, single mothers, mothers of colour, and every other mother whose experience is not already documented in commercials, parenting magazines, and subway advertisements will be relegated, once again, yet more completely, to the margins. Yet from those cyborg margins emerges a story of motherhood that is potentially outside patriarchal motherhood, that, in its irrelevance to public relations executives, is able to be narrated more authentically; in this confusion, power is both exercised and withdrawn. This confusion of power can similarly be seen in the tensions of the mamasphere and blogosphere's hybrid diversity and overall uneven representation.

While I hope that mothers continue to document their personal experiences online, I am also intrigued by the ways that shifts away from the intimate mommyblogs under discussion here might confound traditional ideas about men's and women's writing. Monetized writing, at its best, also confounds ideas about life writing versus marketing, perhaps allowing for a hybrid genre to emerge that editorializes personal details in order to provide marketing support. Such a hybrid has a great potential for misuse but ultimately might result in a style of writing that allows more people from less established positions to participate in marketing; at the very least, such a method has the capacity to be less covert than the focus groups and targeted marketing of the past.

Moving Forward

Given the rapid rise of the mamasphere, it is difficult to imagine where it will go next and what the implications of the mountain of words about motherhood archived online will be, for mothers and for children – as present subjects and as future parents looking back. Bella Brodzki and Celeste Schenck (1988) suggest that "to become a feminist reader of autobiography is to become a new kind of subject" (p. 3). I find myself altered as both a reader and a researcher of mommyblogs; I see in the mamasphere the ways that the endless immediate reactions of life online are shifting the ways mothers live and parent. Many of us are truly transformed by cyberculture, yet this transformation is neither easy nor consistent. As Brodzki and Schenck write,

> the poetics of women's autobiography issues from its concern with constituting a female subject – a precarious operation, which . . . requires working on two fronts at once, *both* occupying a kind of center, assuming a subjectivity long denied, *and* maintaining the vigilant, disruptive stance that speaking from the postmodern margin provides. (1988, p. 286)

Mommyblogging can thus be seen as more than simply a new tool or a new genre – it is a different way of conceiving of the self. In its hybridity, the cyborg connection, the queer mother – in exposing mothers' lives so completely – mothers, and others, are shifted. In participating in a relational medium, detailing a relational practice, the seeds of a relational society may be born. Yet perhaps such an analysis is too pat, too deterministic, and too idealistic to constrain this forum of messiness and complexity.

As Sandra Burt and Lorraine Code (1995) suggest, "Even the most forceful and private of experiences often needs careful interpretation, especially to reveal its embeddedness within larger social patterns, hence, to make it possible to see how, indeed, it is mediated by the circumstances of an experiencer's biographical and social-cultural location" (p. 36). The mamasphere is exceedingly difficult to subject to the kind of careful interpretation suggested by Code and Burt. Its vastness, its web of relationships and links, and its polyvocality all work against any linear method of analysis. Yet it is precisely in its unwieldiness that the mamasphere's great gifts are found: its focus on connection, its commitment to contradiction, and the emergence of a multitudinous clamour instead of a cogent analysis. The mamasphere can shift how we think about motherhood and beyond motherhood in forcing us to truly process the sheer multiplicity of opinions and positions available on any given topic. As we see motherhood from the inside out, our understanding of mothers is forever shifted.

The Changing Face of Motherhood

In thinking and writing about the mamasphere, I've spent a great deal of time explaining what the mamasphere does and how it accomplishes what it accomplishes. This leaves an open question: Why should we care about mommyblogs at all?

In researching this topic, I've consistently received two very distinct responses when I reveal that I study mommyblogs. The first response is generally characterized by a vaguely uncomfortable smile and the sentence "mommyblogs . . . are those a . . . thing?" Many people are completely unaware that mothers are blogging, or that there are internal controversies and endless discussions emerging between mothers online. The second response, however, results in an immediate kinship with the person with whom I am speaking. We immediately trade favourite blogs, connect over people we both follow, and generally launch into complicated insider conversation about bloggers as though they're people we really know. And of course, that's what draws me to this topic: we as readers *do* know them. We just don't know them in a way that is consistent with a traditional means of knowing.

I know that Julia is fabulously creative and loves her twins deeply, even as they drive her to distraction. I know about Heather's recent separation from her partner and her anxieties about a life in flux. I watched Gina from *The Feminist Breeder*'s live video blog of her home birth. How can I know this much about so many and still not have this count as real knowledge? To phrase the question differently, if these are not my friends – yet not strangers – then what is our relationship and why does it matter?

I read mommyblogs because I'm fascinated by the incredible permutations of motherhood and because they make me feel less alone. They give me something distinct from my friendships and enrich my life enormously. This breadth and diversity – the sheer volume of the mamasphere and the resulting diversity of mothering practice captured therein – are what I have termed as hybrid in this book. This hybridity is immensely compelling to me as a hybrid subject. I am an Arab Jew, a brown mother to white children, a straight-seeming queer ally, and a mother/scholar. I live in the margins, in the contradictions. Since my corporeal body, including but not limited to my experiences as a mother, disrupts stability and embodies liminality, the hybrid aspects of the mamasphere validate and confirm my own mess of confusion and incoherence.

For people who are not blog people – the "is that a thing" contingent – the notion that online connections, especially those that are not developed into more traditional friendships, can be nourishing and affirming, never mind theoretically valid, is seen as laughable at best and pitiable at worst, evidence that we are so very starved for "real" relationships that we can only scrabble after the table scraps of companionship that the Internet offers. By contrast, what is evident in reading through the mamasphere is the answer to that elusive "who cares": the notion that digital media and specifically mommyblogs allow for a completely different way of interacting and knowing that does not supplant the need for in-person relationships, but may, nonetheless, allow for an understanding of mothering work in a whole new and unexpected way. Put more bluntly, I have lots of "real" friends, but I still need mommyblogs.

This new way of interacting is what I've termed the cyborg: the notion that in this new way of knowing and not knowing one another mommybloggers have created a whole new conception of support and community. In the endless dialogue that mommyblogs create there is a very supple and mutable picture of motherhood emerging, one that highlights the space between mothers, the space that is easy to ignore in more traditional mothering contexts. Furthermore, the capacity of the Internet to let us play with time lets us talk to our past and future selves and those of others, to use technology to bend time and thus threaten certainty in the very best possible way.

Is this reason enough to care? Do mommyblogs truly present, in their incoherence, a potential for radical change? If we are considering "radical" as a corollary for activist, or as a source for immediate political engagement, then we cannot see the mamasphere as a particularly radical space. It is too insular, too homogeneous, and, while there are wildly diverse and deeply political spaces within the mamasphere, it is overall too concerned with individual matters and not concerned enough, on the whole, with societal change. Considering a shifted understanding of "radical," however, creates the possibility for a new understanding of the mamasphere that has a deep potential for understanding both motherhood and activism in exciting ways. Specifically, the mamasphere shows us a way of supporting one another in an endless web of relations and diversities that only function to shift our understanding of motherhood if taken as a massive organic identity. It is precisely because it is impossible to say anything generalizable about the mamasphere as a whole that it *is* a radical maternal space; not as a result of the activism of individual mothers, but because of the implications of all these narratives coexisting, and the endless unspooling dialogue that therefore emerges.

Traditional activism begins from a premise of "mothers want . . ." or "mothers demand . . ." The activism of the mamasphere, by contrast, answers the question of "what do mothers want?" with a resounding "I don't know," or perhaps with a clamour of competing ideas that drown one another out soundly. This is potentially troubling from the perspective of traditional activism. I have been asked repeatedly throughout this research how mommyblogs improve the lives of mothers. In the final analysis, however, I believe this to be the wrong question. Mommyblogs present a different motherhood, a hybrid, cyborg, and queer motherhood that (sometimes almost despite itself) resists any notion of "mothers are . . ." and therefore cannot respond to what "mothers want." Such an understanding borrows from queer theory, suggesting that all that can be said of this innovative maternal subjectivity is that it isn't any one thing, and that it isn't normative. In precisely the ways that queer theory allows for a slipperiness of identity that foregrounds diversity of both subject and practice, the mamasphere makes mothers and motherhood unidentifiable.

If we don't know who mothers are, how can we fix things? How do we respond to all the limitations and frustrations of patriarchal motherhood that feminist motherhood scholars have spent decades exposing? Rather than trying to fix things for mothers, we need to consider the ways that the mamasphere allows new ways of knowing, and perhaps unknowing, motherhood. Unknowing motherhood looks at the sum total of our capacity to live in the margins rather than the centre, in the relationship rather than the individual, to resist a reckoning of motherhood that is not merely patriarchal, but grandiose. The unity that motherhood activism requires is based on a fundamentally false coherence. An unknowing motherhood such as that presented by the mamasphere splits apart the notion of a totalizing motherhood that can be met by one, or few, forms of activism in favour of a convoluted and fractured chorus of responses and connections.

The mamasphere thus presents a whole new way of envisioning motherhood, the relationships between mothers, the relationships between mothers and their children, and the maternal subject position. While the platitude that it takes a village to raise a child has seemed outdated in an era of self-sufficiency and the idealized nuclear family, the wonder of the Internet has allowed for the creation of an alternate village model that does not require mothers to always agree, that resists the need for ground rules and instead embraces chaos and laughter, loud fervent conversation, and noisy battles. In this respect, the mamasphere as much resembles as reflects family life. A hybrid, cyborg, and queer reckoning of motherhood allows a new theoretical model that seriously engages with Baxter's transformative agenda, looking for what is compelling instead of what is true, looking at the endless multiplicity of mothers instead of their common characteristics. Such a model asks mothers to learn from their children, to indulge in the *play* of identities and relationships over the limitations of their serious and stodgy fixity.

Appendix: List of Blogs Selected for Primary Research

Author's note: The ephemeral nature of the blogosphere means that blogs and their URLs are unstable. As a result, while these are the web addresses that are presently available for these blogs, they may shift or disappear over time.

3 Boys and a Dog (now defunct) – http://momof3boys3702.blogspot.com/
5 Little Monkeys (now password protected) – http://momgoincrazy
   .blogspot.com/
About the Small Stuff – http://aboutthesmallstuff.blogspot.com/
ACU's, Stiletto Shoes, and Pretty Pink Tutus – http://welovelucymichaela
   .blogspot.com/
Adorable Device of Destruction – http://www.adod.blogspot.com/
Adventures of a Passionista – http://www.judeswords.typepad.com/
The Adventures of Eli – http://bigjohnsgirl77.blogspot.com/
The Adventures of Lactating Girl – http://theadventuresoflactatinggirl.com/
The (After) Life of the Party – http://lifeinthelo.blogspot.com/
Aimeepalooza (now password protected) – http://aimeepalooza.blogspot
   .com/
Amalah – http://www.amalah.com/
And Miles to Go Before I Sleep (now password protected) – http:
   //brewerfamily8.blogspot.com/
Anne Nahm – http://annenahm.com/
Another Chapter – http://jeclark32.blogspot.com/
Antique Mommy – http://antiquemommy.com/
Applejuice4everyone (now password protected) – http://applejuice4everyone
   .wordpress.com/

Are You Kidding Me?!?! – http://floriakidz.blogspot.com/
As the Nest Empties – http://www.asthenestempties.blogspot.com/
Attack of the Redneck Mommy – http://www.theredneckmommy.com/
Baby Making Machine – http://www.babymakingmachine.com/
Bad Mom – http://www.thebadmom.com/
Be the Change/The Two Anhs (now password protected) – http://christine-
    bethechange.blogspot.com/
Becoming Mom (now defunct) – http://thepunz.blogspot.com/
Belly Blogs – http://bellyblogs.blogspot.com/
Biblical Homemaking – http://biblicalhomemaking.blogspot.com/
Bitch Ph.D. – http://bitchphd.blogspot.com/
Bittersweet – http://bittersweet.blog.com
Black and Married with Kids – http://blackandmarriedwithkids.com/
Blissfully Beguiling – http://liamack.blogspot.com/
BlogRhet (now defunct) – http://blogrhet.blogspot.com/
Blokthoughts – http://blokthoughtsnmore.blogspot.com/
Blooming Yaya (now password protected) – http://www.bloomingyaya.com/
Blue Milk – http://bluemilk.wordpress.com/
Boogers and Burps – http://www.boogersandburps.com/
Breezy Mama – http://breezymama.com/
Bringing Up Ben and Birdy (on *Babycenter.com*) – http://www.babycenter
    .com/bringing-up-ben-birdy
B'Twixt and B'Tween – http://www.btwixtandbtween.typepad.com/
Bubbalu (now defunct) – http://bubbalulu.com/blog/
But Not for Lunch – http://www.butnotforlunch.blogspot.com/
Cali Dad – http://www.cali-dad.com/
Caring for Carleigh – http://www.caringforcarleigh.com/
Cause for Alarm (now password protected) – http://causeforalarm.wordpress
    .com/
A Celebration of Our Journey (now defunct) – http://acelebrationofour-
    journey.squarespace.com/
Chase(n) Kids (now defunct) – http://chasenkids.org/
Chocolate Party – http://chocolate-party.blogspot.com/
Chookooloonks – http://www.chookooloonks.com/blog/
City Mama – http://citymama.typepad.com/
CJane Enjoy It (now *C.Jane Kendrick*) – http://www.cjanekendrick.com/
Cold Noodles for Breakfast (now defunct) – http://coldnoodlesforbreakfast
    .blogspot.com/
Confessions of a (Not So) Domestic Diva – http://confessionsofanotso-
    domesticdiva.blogspot.com/

Core Foundations – http://corefoundations.wordpress.com/
Crazed Parent – http://www.crazedparent.org/
Crib Ceiling (now password protected) – http://cribceiling.blogspot.com/
Crib Chronicles – http://cribchronicles.com/
Cutest Kid Ever (now *Well, in THIS House...*) – http://wellinthishouse.com
Dalai Mama Dishes (on Disneyfamily.com) – http://family.go.com/blog/
   catherinewman/
Dandelion Dayz – http://www.dandeliondayz.com/
A Day in the Life of a Disabled Mom – http://dayinthelifeofadisabledmom
   .blogspot.com/
A Deaf Mom Shares Her World – http://deafmomworld.com/
Death by Chickens – http://deathbychickens.blogspot.com/
Devis with Babies – http://deviswithbabies.blogspot.com/
Diary of an Unlikely Housewife (now *Globetrotting in Heels*) – http://www
   .theunlikelyhousewife.com/
Distract Me with Shiny Things (now defunct) – http://www.distractme
   withshinythings.com/
The Dominatrix Next Door (now *Dead Cow Girl*) – http://deadcowgirl.com/
Don't Gel Too Soon – http://dontgelyet.typepad.com/dontgeltoosoon/
Dooce – http://www.dooce.com/
Double the Adventure – http://www.doubletheadventure.com/
Dream Mom – http://dreammom.blogspot.com/
Eclectic Effervescence – http://eclecticeffervescence.blogspot.com/
Enchanted Garden Studio – http://whimsicalwitch.blogspot.com/
Et Al. – http://etaliac.blogspot.com/
Eve Dropped Her Basket – http://www.evedroppedherbasket.blogspot.com/
Evolving Mommy – http://www.evolvingmommy.com/
Faith Fuel – http://championyourdreams.blogspot.com/
FannFare – http://www.fannfare.com/
Feminist Childbirth Studies – http://adoulatoo.blogspot.com/
Fickle Feline – http://www.ficklefeline.ca/
Finnian's Journey – http://finniansjourney.blogspot.com/
Finslippy – http://www.finslippy.com/
Florida Girl in Sydney – http://www.floridagirlinsydney.com/
Flotsam – http://flotsamblog.com/
Friday Playdate (now *The Working Closet*) – http://fridayplaydate.com/
A Frog in My Soup – http://afroginmysoup.com/
Front Porch – http://frontporch112.blogspot.com/
Fussy – http://www.fussy.org/
Gaza Mom – http://www.gazamom.com/

Geisha School Dropout – http://geishaschooldropout.typepad.com/
GirlyFruFrus Journey – http://msjena64.blogspot.com/
Gogugo – http://gogugo.blogspot.com/
Gorillabuns – http://www.gorillabuns.typepad.com/
Grace Goes Thru Life – http://gracegoesthrulife.blogspot.com/
Groovy Gams – http://groovygams.blogspot.com/
Gwendomama – http://gwendomama.blogspot.com/
Haas Family Blessings (now defunct) – http://haasfamilyblessings.blogspot
    .com/
Happily Ever After (now password protected) – http://www.nprfl.blogspot
    .com/
Happy Muslim Mama – http://www.happymuslimah.com/
A Hen and Two Chicks – http://www.ahenandtwochicks.blogspot.com/
Her Able Hands – http://herablehands.com/
Her Bad Mother – http://herbadmother.com/
Homesick Home – http://thehomesickhome.blogspot.com/
Home/Work (on *Babble.com*) – http://blogs.babble.com/babble-voices/
    home-work/
An Honest Try (now defunct) – http://anhonesttry.blogspot.com/
Hypergraffiti – http://www.hypergraffiti.com/
I Am Bossy – http://www.iambossy.com/
I Have Things – http://ihavethings.blogspot.com/
In Need of Mercy – http://inneedofmercy.blogspot.com/
Insomnimom – http://www.insomnimom.blogspot.com/
Is It Monday Already? – http://www.isitmondayalready.com/
Is There Any Mommy Out There? – http://www.anymommyoutthere.com/
It's Come to This – http://mlbh.wordpress.com/
Jen on the Edge – http://jenontheedge.com/
Jocelyn's Corner – http://www.filthyrichmond.com/
Journey's [sic] of an Artist Mom – http://apaintersmind.blogspot.com/
Journeys of a Restless Mind – http://ninaturns40.blogs.com/destinations/
J's Thoughts and Musings – http://jennymcb.blogspot.com/
Just Another Day – http://objustanotherday.blogspot.com/
Just My Life (now *Random Ramblings*) – http://www.threeintwoyears
    .blogspot.com/
The Karianna Spectrum – http://www.karianna.us/blog/
Kelly's Korner – http://www.kellyskornerblog.com/
Kimchi Mamas – http://kimchimamas.typepad.com/
Kim + Eddie = Ki-ddie – http://kimpluseddie.wordpress.com/
Knotted – http://knotted.typepad.com/knotted/

La Mama – http://llamama.blogspot.com/
Larger Family Life – http://www.largerfamilylife.com/
Lesbian Dad – http://www.lesbiandad.net/
Letters from Home – http://caliphoenix.wordpress.com/
Life As I Know It   http://lifeaiknowit.blogspot.com/
Life, Liberty, & Vodka Tonics – http://lifelibertyvodkatonics.blogspot.com/
Life with the Cuties – http://cutiefaces.blogspot.com/
Little Baby Lump – http://littlebabylump.com/
A Little Bit of Everything – http://amywing.wordpress.com/
A Little of This a Little of That – http://www.kyrepomanager.blogspot.com/
A Little Pregnant – http://www.alittlepregnant.com/
Live from the Wang of America – http://livefromthewangofamerica.blogspot
    .com/
Looked Good on Paper – http://lookedgoodonpaper.com/
Love Letters from Mommy – http://lovelettersfrommommy.blogspot.com/
Lucy the Valiant – http://queenlucythevaliant.blogspot.com
Mad, Mad Mama – http://madmadmama.com/
Making It Fun – http://happytogetherish.blogspot.com/
Mamadrama (on *Chron.com*) – http://blogs.chron.com/mamadrama/
Mamalicious – http://www.mamaliciousnoire.com/
MamaPop – http://www.mamapop.com/
Mamapundit – http://mamapundit.com/
Mama's Cup – http://www.mamascup.com/
Manager Mommy – http://managermommy.blogspot.com/
Marie Millard – http://www.mariemillard.blogspot.com/
Mathers, Party of 4 – http://www.matherspartyof3.blogspot.com/
Meandering Threads – http://meanderingthreads.blogspot.com/
Military Mommie – http://militarymommie.blogspot.com/
Mimi Smartypants – http://mimismartypants.com/
MK Stover – http://www.mkstover.com/
Momathon – http://momathonblog.typepad.com/momathon_blog/
A Moment in Time (now password protected) – http://www.origazgirl
    .blogspot.com/
Mommy Brain Life – http://www.mommybrainlife.com/
Mommy Melee – http://mommymelee.com/
Mommy Needs Coffee – http://www.mommyneedscoffee.com/
Mommypalooza – http://www.mommypalooza.com/
Mommy Sanctuary – http://mommysanctuary.blogspot.com/
Mommy's Time Out (now defunct) – http://banocyfamily.blogspot.com/
The Mom Slant (now defunct) – http://www.themomslant.com/

Momsoon – http://momsoon.blogspot.com/

Mom Tips and Notes from the Zoo (now defunct) – http://shmopsmomtips
  .blogspot.com/

Moogie's World – http://moogiesworld.com/

Motherhood Uncensored – http://motherhooduncensored.typepad.com/

Mother Inferior – http://www.denadyer.typepad.com/

Motherwise Cracks – http://motherwise.us/cracks/

Mrs. Fussypants (now defunct) – http://mrsfussypants.com/

Mundane Musings – http://mundanemusings.com/

Musings – http://mamagigi.wordpress.com/

Musings Musings Musings (now password protected) – http://musings-
  musings-musings.blogspot.com/

My Big Fat Blog (now defunct) – http://momwifesuperhero.blogspot.com/

My Favorite Things – http://www.irwinagnes.blogspot.com/

My Life As "Momma" – http://marmarbug-mylifeasmomma.blogspot.com/

My Life of What Ifs – http://www.mylifeofwhatifs.com/

My Mommy Rocks! – http://ldrmommyrocks.blogspot.com/

My Sacred Journey – http://momofboys-tracy.blogspot.com/

Naked on Roller Skates – http://nancybartholomew.blogspot.com/

NaturallyEstes – http://naturallyestes.blogspot.com/

New Mummy – http://mummynew.blogspot.com/

North Side Four – http://northsidefour.blogspot.com/

Not Your Mother's Weblog – http://blogbrarian.wordpress.com/

Nouvelle Blogger – http://www.nouvelleblogger.blogspot.com/

Only This – http://www.ericandjamie.com/blogs/jamie/

On Stage – http://on-stage-in-valpo.blogspot.com/

Other People's Poop (now defunct) – http://mpoop.blogspot.com/

Owlhaven – http://www.owlhaven.net/

Peter's Cross Station – http://peterscrossstation.wordpress.com/

PhD in Parenting – http://www.phdinparenting.com/

Pint Sized Explorers (now defunct) – http://www.pintsizeexplorers.com/

A Place Called Good – http://aplacecalledgood.com/

Pocket Lint – http://www.mypocketlint.blogspot.com/

A Poor Mom's Blog – http://ifoundhome.wordpress.com/

Psychobabbling – http://psychobabbling.net/

Ravings of a Mad Housewife – http://www.ravingsofamadhousewife.com/

Real Heart Prints – http://missmalu30.blogspot.com/

The Renegade Rebbetzin (now password protected) – http://renegade
  rebbetzin.blogspot.com/

Room on the Counter (now password protected) – http://roomonthecounter
    .blogspot.com/
Royal (A Queen in Training) (now defunct) – http://aqueenintraining
    .blogspot.com/
Ryter Rytes – http://ryterrytes.wordpress.com/
Salty Momma – http://www.saltymomma.com/
Sanity vs. 4 Kids – http://sanityvs4kids.blogspot.com/
Seattle Jo – http://seattlejo.com/
Shebazzle – http://shebazzle.com/
Sicker than Others – http://www.sickerthanothers.com/
Simple Little Home – http://simplelittlehome.blogspot.com/
Skwishface – http://skwishface.wordpress.com/
Somewhere in the Suburbs – http://somewhereinthesuburbs.wordpress.com/
So the Fish Said . . . – http://www.sothefishsaid.com/
Southwest Mementoes – http://www.killlashandra.org/wordpress/
Spunky Homeschool – http://www.spunkyhomeschool.blogspot.com/
State of Grace – http://gracedavis.typepad.com/
Steece's Pieces – http://thelifeofsuz.blogspot.com/
The Story Midwife – http://mellamusings.typepad.com/story_midwife/
Sunflower Meadows – http://sunflowermeadow2.blogspot.com/
Swirls in my Head – http://mentalmommy.blogspot.com/
Tales from the Funny Farm (now defunct) – http://talesfromthefunnyfarm
    .blogspot.com/
A Ten O'clock Scholar – http://www.theten0clockscholar.blogspot.com/
That's Empress to You – http://thatsempresstoyou.typepad.com/
Theories of Everything – http://theoriesofeverything.wordpress.com/
This Mom – http://kyraanderson.wordpress.com/
This, That and Everything Else in Between – http://daniellicious.blogspot
    .com/
Tina's Realm – http://www.tinasrealm.blogspot.com/
Total Momsense – http://www.totalmomsense.net/
Transgender Mom – http://transgendermom.blogspot.com/
Typical American Mom (now password protected) – http://momhelen
    .blogspot.com/
Unfit Mutha – http://unfitmutha.blogspot.com/
Unwellness – http://www.unwellness.com/
Up North Mommy (now defunct) – http://kimpriestap.typepad.com/
Vintage Dutch Girl – http://vintagedutchgirl.blogspot.com/
Watch Me! No, Watch Me! (now defunct) – http://www.watchmenowatchme
    .com/

Weebles Weblog (now *Write Mind Open Heart*) – http://writemindopenheart
.com/
Where's My White Picket Fence? – http://wheresmywhitepicketfence
.blogspot.com/
Wonderland (on *Alphamom.com*) – http://alphamom.com/tag/wonderland/
Yarn Harlot – http://www.yarnharlot.ca/blog/
You Just Never Know Where Hope Can Take Ya (now password protected)
– http://canonlyimagine.blogspot.com/
The Young Mommy Life – http://www.theyoungmommylife.com/
Zoloft Mom – http://www.zoloftmom.blogspot.com/

Notes

1. Introduction

1 Catherine Newman, "Camping on the Cape," *Bringing Up Ben and Birdy* (blog), *Babycenter*, July 2002, http://www.babycenter.com/0_bringing-up-ben-week-1-camping-on-the-cape_72451.bc.

2 Mimi Smartypants, "All Female Fertility Festival Associated with Demeter, *Mimi Smartypants*, 2 January 2004, http://mimismartypants.com/2004/01/02/all-female-fertility-festival-associated-with-demeter/.

3 Heather Armstrong, "If This Isn't Reclaiming the Web for Personal Expression then I DON'T KNOW WHAT IS," *Dooce*, 15 June 2005, http://dooce.com/archives/daily/06_15_2005.html.

4 "Thick" narrative borrows from the language of narrative therapy and suggests that, "The thin truths proposed by . . . power figure[s] have been replaced by the convincing rich or thick actuality of the person's lived experience and consciously held knowledge" (Payne, 2006, 36).

5 Catherine Newman, "Plum Cake," *Dalai Mama Dishes* (blog), *Disney Family*, 13 October 2008, http://family.go.com/blog/catherinewman/plum-cake-690752/.

6 "Bulletin board system," *Wikipedia*, last modified 12 June 2012, http://en.wikipedia.org/wiki/Bulletin_board_system.

7 While it is exceptionally difficult to accurately count mommyblogs, most estimates suggest there are millions. For example, emarketer.com estimates that, as of October 2010, 3.9 million women with children are blogging, and that the number is expected to rise to 4.4 million by 2014 ("Blog Marketing to Moms Is About More Than Parenting," *Emarketer*, 8 October 2010, http://www.emarketer.com/Article.aspx?R=1007976).

8 The term "digital divide," defined as "the troubling gap between those who use computers and the Internet and those who do not" (Mehra et al., 2004, p. 782), initially referred only to computer ownership; as Internet use has become more firmly embedded in the details of Western life, it has become a core component of the digital divide. Bharat Mehra et al. argue that race, class and education are the key components that disallow some people from digital citizenry. These characteristics generally refer to a digital divide within industrialized nations, looking, for example, at the increased computer and web access that wealthy students might receive over their poorer counterparts. Beyond this definition, however, there is an increasing discussion of the global digital divide, the lack of computer hardware and digital infrastructure that leaves much of the developing world unconnected.

9 Among the most famous Internet hoaxes was one that involved a young woman named Kaycee Nicole presenting herself as a cancer patient. After Kaycee's "death," it became clear that the woman presented in the blog as her mother had created the entire narrative and that Kaycee Nicole was entirely fictitious ("Kaycee Nicole," *Wikipedia*, last modified 16 June 2012, http://en.wikipedia.org/wiki/Kaycee_Nicole). Similar cases have since been collected under the umbrella term "Münchausen by Internet."

10 VNS Matrix, "Cyberfeminist Manifesto," http://www.sysx.org/gashgirl/ VNS/TEXT/PINKMANI.HTM.

2. A Short History of the Mamasphere and the Discursive Construction of Motherhood

1 Molly Westerman, "No Cheese For You," *Feminist Childbirth Studies*, October 2009, http://adoulatoo.blogspot.com/ (post has been deleted).

2 Phillip Win, "State of the Blogosphere 2008: Introduction," *Technorati*, 21 August 2009, http://technorati.com/social-media/article/ state-of-the-blogosphere-introduction/.

3 "Buzz in the Blogosphere: Millions More Bloggers and Blog Readers," *nielsenwire*, 8 March 2012, http://blog.nielsen.com/nielsenwire/online_mobile/ buzz-in-the-blogosphere-millions-more-bloggers-and-blog-readers/.

4 Phillip Win, "State of the Blogosphere 2008: Introduction," *Technorati*, 21 August 2009, http://technorati.com/social-media/article/ state-of-the-blogosphere-introduction/.

5 Eden Marriott Kennedy, *Fussy*, 31 January 2005, http://www.fussy. org/2005/01/766.html.

6 Kyra Anderson, "That Article," *This Mom*, 30 January 2005, http://thismom .blogs.com/this_mom/2005/01/i_read_david_ho.html.

7   Lisa Stone, "Celebrate BlogHer's 5th Anniversary With Us and Win One of Five Free Passes With #BlogHer5," *BlogHer*, 20 January 2010, http://www .blogher.com/celebrate-bloghers-5th-anniversary-us-and-win-one-five- free-passes-blogher5.

8   Jennifer Satterwhite, "Mommybloggers: Integrity, Community and Taking Back the Respect We Earned," *Mommy Needs Coffee*, 1 August 2009, http:// mommyneedscoffee.com/2009/08/mommybloggers-respect/.

9   Ibid.

10 Elisa Camahort, "BlogHer '06 Session Discussion: MommyBlogging is a Radical Act! on Day Two," *BlogHer*, 20 May 2006, http://www.blogher.com/ node/5563.

11 Jennifer Satterwhite, "Mommybloggers: Integrity, Community and Taking Back the Respect We Earned," *Mommy Needs Coffee*, 1 August 2009, http:// mommyneedscoffee.com/2009/08/mommybloggers-respect/.

3. On Hybridity

1   Catherine Connor, "Ten Things I Hate About Motherhood (and One that I Love," *Her Bad Mother*, 20 April 2010, http://herbadmother. com/2010/04/10-things-i-hate-about-motherhood-and-one-that-i-love/.

2   Laila El-Haddad, "Gaza, My City," *Gaza Mom*, 22 February 2010, http:// www.gazamom.com/2010/02/gaza-my-city/.

3   Tara Pringle Jefferson, "About Me," *The Young Mommy Life*, November 9, 2009, http://www.theyoungmommylife.com/about/.

4   Tara Pringle Jefferson, "Where Have You Been All My Life?" *The Young Mommy Life*, 3 November 2009, http://www.theyoungmommylife. com/2009/11/03/where-have-you-been-all-my-life/.

5   Deepa, "To Blog or Not to Blog – Or Why You Should Read This Blog," *Devies with Babies*, 18 September 2008, http://deviswithbabies.blogspot .ca/2008/09/to-blog-or-not-to-blog-or-why-you.html.

6   Deepa, "Obama, One Week Later," *Devis with Babies*, 10 November 2008, http://deviswithbabies.blogspot.ca/2008/11/obama-one-week-later.html.

7   "Best. Babyshower. Ever!" *The Dominatrix Next Door*, 19 Feburary 2009, http://deadcowgirl.com/2009/02/best-babyshower-ever/.

8   "Meet Me at the Crossroads," *The Dominatrix Next Door*, 30 December 2008, http://deadcowgirl.com/2008/12/meet-me-at-the-crossroads/.

9   *The Renegade Rebbetzin*, January 2007, http://renegaderebbetzin.blogspot .com/ (now password protected).

10 *The Renegade Rebbetzin*, 24 November 2009, http://renegaderebbetzin .blogspot.com/ (now password protected).

11 "First Post!" *Transgender Mom*, 1 November 2008, http://transgendermom .blogspot.ca/2008/11/first-post_01.html.

12 "About de-transitioning," *Transgender Mom*, 17 April 2009, http://trans-gendermom.blogspot.ca/2009/04/about-detransitioning.html.

13 "Thoughts on Someone Who Didn't Go through with Transition," *Trans-gender Mom*, 19 April 2009, http://transgendermom.blogspot.ca/2009/04/ thoughts-on-someone-who-didnt-go.html.

14 Briar, "More Boob Thoughts from Playgroup," *Unwell-ness*, 9 December 2008, http://unwellness.com/2008/12/09/ more-alternathoughts-from-playgroup/.

15 Briar, "I Like to Work," *Unwellness*, 17 June 2010, http://unwellness .com/2010/06/17/i-like-to-work/.

16 "I Can See All Obstacles in My Way," *Fannfare*, 25 June 2008, http://www .fannfare.com/?p=428.

17 Susan, "About," *Friday Playdate*, accessed 11 June 2010, http://friday playdate.blogspot.com.

18 Sue Hood, "Aspiring to Give Great Care, Taking Parenting to the Next Level," *Dream Mom*, 1 July 2009, http://dreammom.blogspot.ca/2009/06/ aspiring-to-give-great-care-taking.html.

19 Gidge, "Bowling Champions of a Sort," *Live from the Wang of America*, 25 January 2010, http://livefromthewangofamerica.blogspot.ca/2010/01/ bowling-champions-of-sort.html.

20 Gidge, "The Road to Gattica is Paved with These," *Live from the Wang of America*, 15 December 2009, http://livefromthewangofamerica.blogspot .ca/2009/12/road-to-gattica-is-paved-with-these.html.

21 Shannon LC Cate, "Octuplets = Bad Mother Ideology x Eight," *Peter's Cross Station*, 16 February 2009, http://peterscrossstation.wordpress .com/2009/02/16/octuplets-bad-mother-ideology-x-eight/.

22 Stacey Conner, "She's a Butterfly," *Any Mommy Out There?* 15 June 2010, http://anymommyoutthere.com/2010/06/shes-butterfly.html.

23 Stacey Conner, "Disruption: A Failed Mom's Look Back," *Any Mommy Out There?* 10 July 2008, http://anymommyoutthere.com/2008/07/ disruption-failed-moms-look-back.html.

24 The entire list of blogs referred to in this book can be found in Appendix A.

25 Interestingly, after five years of this description, Armstrong now refers to herself as a professional blogger instead. Perhaps of even more interest, reflecting the impermanence of the Internet, Armstrong's former self-description has now vanished and will, within a short period of time, no longer exist as a historical artefact of her prior self-identification.

4. On the Cyborg

1 Stephanie Pearl-McPhee, "Six," *Yarn Harlot*, 23 January 2010, http://www
.yarnharlot.ca/blog/archives/2010_01.html.
2 Bonnie Stewart, "The Cyborg Momifesto," *Crib Chronicles*, 23 June 2009,
http://cribchronicles.com/2009/06/23/the-cyborg-momifesto/.
3 Kathy, "To Boldly Go Where No Gams Has Gone Before," *Groovy Gams*,
29 May 2009, http://groovygams.blogspot.ca/2009/05/to-boldly-go-where-
no-gams-has-gone.html.
4 Julie Robichaux, "If the Prize Is a Leg Lamp, I Really Hope I Win,"
A Little Pregnant, 18 June 2010, http://www.alittlepregnant.com/
alittlepregnant/2010/06/for-now-just-one-sentence-about-tyler-place-i-
dont-know-what-the-best-part-is-that-their-group-leaders-take-our-kids-
to-th.html.
5 Stacey Conner, "Let's Talk About Transracial International Adoption," *Any
Mommy Out There?* 24 May 2008, http://anymommyoutthere.com/2008/05/
lets-talk-about-transracial.html.
6 "Hello Chickens, Have You Come Home to Roost?" *Blue Milk*,
28 November 2007, http://bluemilk.wordpress.com/2007/11/28/
hello-chickens-have-you-come-home-to-roost/.
7 Catherine Connors, "Are They Reinventing Motherhood (or just giving us
a sneak peak [sic] into previously private journals)?" *BlogRhet*, 16 February
2008 http://blogrhet.blogspot.ca/2008/02/are-they-reinventing-motherhood-
or-just.html.
8 "In the Wild West You Need to Gather a Posse," *Blue Milk*,
21 August 2007, http://bluemilk.wordpress.com/2007/08/21/
in-the-wild-west-you-need-to-gather-a-posse/.
9 Bobita, "With Much Gratitude," *Blooming Yaya*, 2 August 2006, http://www
.bloomingyaya.com (now password protected).
10 Lisa Morguess, "Impact," *Finnian's Journey*, 31 October 2009, http://
finniansjourney.blogspot.ca/2009/10/impact.html.
11 Courtney Jane Kendrick, "FAQ of the Matter," *CJane Enjoy It*, 13 June 2010,
http://www.cjanekendrick.com/2010/06/faq-of-matter.html.
12 Lucy, "The Dark Underbelly of Motherhood. Now With Pictures!" *Lucy
the Valiant*, 26 July 2009, http://queenlucythevaliant.blogspot.ca/2009/07/
dark-underbelly-of-motherhood-now-with.html.
13 Catherine Connors, "So Jesus, Socrates and a Blogger Walk into a Bar: Reflections on Being Good in the Internet Age," *Her Bad Mother*, 14 January
2010, http://herbadmother.com/causes/so-jesus-socrates-and-a-blogger-
walk-into-a-bar-reflections-on-being-good-in-the-internet-age/.

14 Shana, "The doo doo doo. The dah dah dah. All I want to say to you," *Gorillabuns*, 7 July 2009, http://gorillabuns.typepad.com/my_weblog/ 2009/07/the-doo-doo-doo-the-dah-dah-dah-all-i-want-to-say-to-you .html.

15 Shana "Vindication," *Gorillabuns*, 2 September 2009, http://gorillabuns. typepad.com/my_weblog/2009/09/iamvery-relunctant-in-writing-this- post-as-i-will-probably-gather-all-sorts-of-crazy-folk-as-i-am-wont-to-do- but-i-am-going-t.html.

16 Stacey Conner, "The Obligatory Blog Post about Blogging," *Any Mommy Out There?* 3 August 2008, http://anymommyoutthere.com/2008/08/obliga- tory-blog-post-about-blogging.html.

17 Elisa, "Shut It and Listen," *Diary of an Unlikely Housewife*, 1 July 2009, http://www.theunlikelyhousewife.com/2009/07/shut-it-and-listen/.

18 Tara Pringle Jefferson, "Maternity Picks of the Week, Cute Top Edition," *The Young Mommy Life*," 3 July 2008, http://www.theyoungmommylife .com/2008/07/03/maternity-picks-of-the-week-cute-top-edition/.

19 The "autobiographical contract," originally put forth by Philippe Lejeune, suggests that autobiography ought to be a "narrative produced by a real person concerning his own existence, focusing on his individual life, in particular on the development of his [sic] personality" (1982, p. 193).

20 Heather Armstrong of *Dooce*, Alice Bradley of *Finslippy*, Eden Marriott Kennedy of *Fussy*, and Catherine Connors of *Her Bad Mother* are the spe- cific popular mommybloggers discussed in this analysis.

21 Alice Bradley, "A Few Words about Fear," *Finslippy*, 29 January 2010, http://www.finslippy.com/blog/2010/1/29/a-few-words-about-fear.html.

22 Heather Armstrong, "Your Momma Said You Ugly," *Dooce*, 16 September 2009, http://dooce.com/2009/09/16/your-momma-said-you-ugly/.

23 Heather Armstrong, "Monetizing the Hate," *Dooce*, accessed 11 November 2010, http://dooce.com/hate/.

24 Julie Robichaux, "Breastfeeding Is Awesome. There. I've Encouraged You," *A Little Pregnant*, 4 August 2010, http://www.alittlepregnant.com/ alittlepregnant/2010/08/breastfeeding-is-awesome-there-ive-encouraged- you.html.

25 Briar, "Blog as Helpful Calendar of Fear and Joy," *Unwellness*, 14 July 2010, http://unwellness.com/2010/07/14/blog-as-helpful-calendar-of-fear-and- joy/.

26 Laura, "It's Complicated," *Florida Girl in Sidney*, 20 June 2008, http://www .floridagirlinsydney.com/2008/06/its-complicated.html.

27 Bonnie Stewart, "The Cyborg Momifesto," *Crib Chronicles*, 23 June 2009, http://cribchronicles.com/2009/06/23/the-cyborg-momifesto/.

28 Alison Hale, "Limbo," *Et Al.*, 5 October 2005, http://etaliae.blogspot
   .ca/2005/10/limbo.html.

29 Julie Kang, "BANANA Peels," *Geisha School Dropout*, 24 November 2009,
   http://geishaschooldropout.typepad.com/geisha_school_dropout/2009/11/
   banana peels 1.html.

30 "About," *Typical American Mom*, accessed 11 May 2010, http://momhelen
   .blogspot.com.

5. On Queer

 1 "Who's Your Daddy (and For That Matter, Your Mummy)?" *Blue
    Milk*, 17 May 2007, http://bluemilk.wordpress.com/2007/05/17/
    whos-your-daddy-and-for-that-matter-your-mummy/.

 2 "Off to Preschool," *Front Porch*, 16 January 2010, http://frontporch112
    .blogspot.ca/2010/01/off-to-preschool.html.

 3 David Gauntlett, "Queer Theory," accessed 18 July 2012, http://www
    .theory.org.uk/ctr-que1.htm.

 4 Not all gay, lesbian, bisexual, and transgendered individuals have em-
    braced the word "queer." For some people with strong affiliations with
    other identity categories, such as lesbian, the abandonment of a specific
    area of identity may feel like a concession, a relinquishing of the political
    power associated with strong collective consciousness.

 5 Elizabeth, "Just Me" *Blogger* Profile, *Making It Fun*, accessed 18 May 2010,
    http://www.blogger.com/profile/09613843318204543298.

 6 Shera, "Balance," *Frog in My Soup*, 31 March 2010, http://afroginmysoup
    .com/2010/balance/.

 7 "Privacy," *Anne Nahm*, 8 June 2006, http://annenahm.com/?p=123.

 8 "Back from Vacation Funk," *Mommy Sanctuary*, 6 August 2008, http://
    mommysanctuary.blogspot.ca/2008/08/back-from-vacation-funk.html.

 9 Annie, "Intersecting Needs: Maslow, Interdependence, Parenting, Care-
    giving, Relationships," *PhD in Parenting*, 20 January 2010, http://www
    .phdinparenting.com/2010/01/20/intersecting-needs-maslow-inter-
    dependence-parenting-caregiving-relationships/.

10 Deesha Philyaw, "Tip #287: Making Long Distance Love Work – Text Game
    Proper," *Mamalicious*, 25 November 2009, http://www.mamaliciousnoire
    .com/2009/11/25/tip-287-making-long-distance-love-work-text-game-proper/.

11 "So, OK," *Bitch Ph.D.*, 12 May 2010 (originally posted in 2005), http://
    bitchphd.blogspot.ca/2010/05/so-ok.html.

12 Deesha Philyaw, "Tip #792: Making Long-Distance Love Work: It's Not All
    Romance and Roses," *Mamalicious*, 7 March 2010, http://www.mama-

.liciousnoire.com/2010/03/07/tip-792-making-long-distance-love-work-its-not-all-romance-roses/.

13 Alice Bradley, "Here's Where I Get All Preachy. You Can Skim This One," *Finslippy*, 20 February 2005, http://www.finslippy.com/blog/heres-where-i-get-all-preachy-you-can-skim-this-one.html.

14 Katie Allison Granju, "Did You Hear the One About the Woman Who Wrote the Book About Breastfeeding Who Isn't Breastfeeding?" *Home/Work* (blog) on *Babble*, 10 August 2010, http://www.babble.com/cs/home-work/2010/08/10/did-you-hear-the-one-about-the-woman-who-wrote-the-book-about-breastfeeding-who-isn-t-breastfeeding/.

15 Maria Mora, "This Is Not a MomCasting Audition," *Mommy Melee*, 26 July 2010, http://mommymelee.com/2010/07/this-is-not-a-momcasting-audition/.

16 Alexa Stevenson, "Five Years," *Flotsam*, 19 July 2010, http://flotsamblog.com/2010/07/19/five-years/.

17 Alice Bradley, following the success of her personal blog, blogged professionally on a parenting site called *Alphamom* from November 2007 to February 2009. These posts can be seen at http://alphamom.com/tag/wonderland/.

18 Alice Bradley, "Writing About Your Kids: A Few Thoughts on Parent Blogging," *Alphamom*, 1 August 2008, http://alphamom.com/your-life/life-relationships/writing-about-your-kids-a-few-thoughts-on-parent-blogging/.

19 Marie, "Conversation Hearts: Blond to the Roots, Dumb Like a Fox," *Marie Millard*, 4 November 2009, http://mariemillard.blogspot.ca/2009/11/conversation-hearts-blonde-to-roots.html.

20 Jessica G., "What Happens When Moms Write Memoirs?" *Jezebel: Celebrity, Sex, Fashion for Women*, 5 December 2008, http://jezebel.com/5102635/what-happens-when-moms-write-memoirs

21 Jane, "From the Feminism, You're Doing It Wrong Files: Jezebel Tells Moms That It Would Be Better, Maybe, If They Just Shut Up," *MamaPop*, 8 December 2008, http://www.mamapop.com/2008/12/from-the-feminism-youre-doing-it-wrong-files-jezebel-tells-moms-that-it-would-be-better-maybe-if-they-just-shut-up.html.

22 Rachel Pastan, "Bad Parent: The Muse – I Exploit My Child for Art," *Babble.com*, 7 May 2008, http://www.babble.com/mom/work-family/rachel-pastan-writing-about-kids-mother-and-daughter-relationship/.

23 Quoted in Alice Bradley, "Writing About Your Kids: A Few Thoughts on Parent Blogging," *Alphamom*, 1 August 2008, http://alphamom.com/your-life/life-relationships/writing-about-your-kids-a-few-thoughts-on-parent-blogging/.

24 Grace Davis, "I Am Dr. Laura's Worst Nightmare," *State of Grace*, 6 July 2009, http://gracedavis.typepad.com/ (now defunct).

25 Heather Armstrong, "Newsletter: Month Fifty and Fifty-one," *Dooce*, 2 May 2008, http://dooce.com/2008/05/02/newsletter-month-fifty-and-fifty-one/.
26 Alice Bradley, "Writing About Your Kids: A Few Thoughts on Parent Blogging," *Alphamom*, 1 August 2008, http://alphamom.com/your-life/life-relationships/writing-about-your-kids-a-few-thoughts-on-parent-blogging/.

6. Conclusion

1 Bonnie Stewart, "The Cruellest Month," Crib Chronicles, 13 April 2009, http://cribchronicles.com/2009/04/13/the-cruellest-month/.
2 "Notes from the Underwire," *Antique Mommy*, 20 July 2009, http://antiquemommy.com/2009/07/20/notes-from-the-underwire/.
3 Jennifer Satterwhite, "Mommybloggers: Integrity, Community and Taking Back the Respect We Earned," *Mommy Needs Coffee*, 1 August 2009, http://mommyneedscoffee.com/2009/08/mommybloggers-respect/.
4 Amalah, "Blogher, Part One," 29 July 2009, http://www.amalah.com/amalah/2009/07/blogher-part-one.html#.UBiQc2jdfIY.
5 Kellie, "My Journey with the Internet," *My Big Fat Blog*, 19 September 2007, http://momwifesuperhero.blogspot.com/ (now defunct).
6 Kellie, "Bush Furniture for Your Home!" *My Big Fat Blog*, 22 September 2007, http://momwifesuperhero.blogspot.com/ (now defunct).
7 Stefania Pomponi Butler, "Putting PR People on Notice, *City Mama*, 28 July 2007, http://citymama.typepad.com/citymama/2007/07/putting-pr-peop.html.

References

Arreola, Veronica I. (2008, May 31). Mommy & Me. *Bitch Magazine.* Retrieved from http://bitchmagazine.org/article/mommy-me

Balsamo, Anne. (1999). *Technologies of the gendered body: Reading cyborg women.* Durham: Duke University Press.

Barlow, Aaron. (2008). *Blogging America: The new public sphere.* Westport: Praeger.

Barthes, Roland. (1977, translated reissue 2006). The death of the author. *Athenaeum library of philosophy.* Retrieved from http://evans-experientialism.free-webspace.com/barthes06.htm

Baumgardner, Jennifer, & Richards, Amy. (2000). *Manifesta: Young women, feminism and the future.* New York: Farrar, Straus and Giroux.

Baxter, Judith. (2002). Is PDA really an alternative? A reply to West. *Discourse & Society, 13*(6), 853–9. http://dx.doi.org/10.1177/0957926502013006762

– (2008). Feminist post-structuralist discourse analysis: A new theoretical and methodological approach? In Kate Harrington, Lia Litosseliti, Helen Saunton, & Jane Sunderland (Eds.), *Gender and language research methodologies* (pp. 243–55). New York: Palgrave.

Bérubé, Michael. (2006). *Rhetorical occasions: Essays on humans and the humanities.* Durham: University of North Carolina Press.

Blood, Rebecca. (2000, September 7). Weblogs: A history and perspective. Retrieved from http://www.rebeccablood.net/essays/weblog_history.html

Bowen, Deborah S. (2009). E-criture feminine: Women's online diaries and the new female discourse. In Kristine Blair, Radhika Gajjala, & Christine Tulley (Eds.), *Webbing cyberfeminist practice: Communities, pedagogies and social action* (pp. 309–26). Cresskill, NJ: Hampton Press.

Brah, Avtar, & Coombes, Annie E. (2000). *Hybridity and its discontents: Politics, science, culture*. London: Routledge.

Bridger, Barbara. (2009). Writing across the borders of the self. *European Journal of Women's Studies, 16*(4), 337–52. doi:10.1177/1350506809342613

Brodzki, Bella, & Schenck, Celeste (Eds.). (1988). *Life/lines: Theorizing women's autobiography*. Ithaca: Cornell University Press.

Burt, Sandra, & Code, Lorraine (Eds.). (1995). *Changing methods: Feminists transforming practice*. Peterborough: Broadview Press.

Butler, Judith. (1990). *Gender trouble: Feminism and the subversion of identity*. New York: Routledge.

– (1993). *Bodies that matter: On the discursive limits of "sex."* New York: Routledge.

Cameron, Deborah. (1998). Gender, language, and discourse: A review essay. *Signs: Journal of women in culture and society, 23*(4), 945–74. http://dx.doi.org/10.1086/495297

Chandler, Daniel. (1998). *Personal Home Pages and the Construction of Identities on the Web*. Retrieved from http://www.aber.ac.uk/media/Documents/short/webident.html.

Chandler, Mielle. (2007). Emancipated subjectivities and the subjugation of mothering practices. In Andrea O'Reilly (Ed.), *Maternal Theory: Essential Readings* (pp. 529–41). Toronto: Demeter Press.

Coleman, Linda S. (1997). *Women's life writing: Finding voice, building community*. Bowling Green: Bowling Green State University Popular Press.

Cusk, Rachel. (2003). *A life's work: On becoming a mother*. New York: Picador.

Davies, Bronwyn, & Gannon, Susanne (Eds.). (2006). *Doing collective biography: Investigating the production of subjectivity*. Maidenhead, UK: McGraw Hill.

de Lauretis, Teresa. (1991). Queer theory: Lesbian and gay sexualities. *differences: A Journal of Feminist Cultural Studies, 3*(2), iii–xviii.

DiQuinzio, Patrice. (1999). *The impossibility of motherhood: Feminism, individualism and the problem of mothering*. New York: Routledge.

Doctorow, Cory. (2003). *Down and out in the magic kingdom*. New York: Tor Books.

Douglas, Susan J., & Michaels, Meredith W. (2004). *The mommy myth: The idealization of motherhood and how it has undermined all women*. New York: The Free Press.

Dubinsky, Karen. (2007). Babies without borders: Rescue, kidnap and the symbolic child. *Journal of Women's History, 19*(1), 142–50. doi:10.1353/jowh.2007.0009

Eakin, Paul John. (1999). *How our lives become stories: Making selves*. Ithaca: Cornell University Press.

Ferris, Lisa. (2009). Kindred keyboard connections: How blogging helped a deafblind mother find a living, breathing community. In May Friedman &

Shana Calixte (Eds.), *Mothering and blogging: The radical act of the mommyblog* (pp. 67–73). Toronto: Demeter Press.

Finke, Laurie A. (1992). *Feminist theory: Women's writing*. Ithaca: Cornell University Press.

Fischer, Hervé. (2006). *Digital shock: Confronting the new reality*. Quebec City: McGill-Queen's University Press.

Foucault, Michel (1976, translated reissue, 1990). *The history of sexuality: An introduction, volume I*. New York: Vintage Books.

– (1980). *Power/knowledge: Selected interviews and other writings, 1972–1977*. New York: Random House.

– (1991). *Governmentality*. In Graham Burchill, Colin Gorden, & Peter Miller (Eds.), *The Foucault effect: Studies in governmentality: With two lectures by and an interview with Michel Foucault* (pp. 87–104). Chicago: University of Chicago Press.

Friedman, May. (2008). "Everything you need to know about your baby": Feminism and attachment parenting. In Jessica Nathanson & Laura Camile Tuley (Eds.), *Mother knows best: Talking back to the "experts"* (pp. 135–47). Toronto: Demeter Press.

Friedman, May & Calixte, Shana L. (Eds.) (2009). *Mothering and blogging: The radical act of the mommyblog*. Toronto: Demeter Press.

Friedman, May, & Schultermandl, Silvia. (2011). *Growing up transnational: Identity and kinship in a global era*. Toronto: University of Toronto Press.

Gilbert, Jennifer. (2009). I kid you not: How the Internet talked me out of traditional mommyhood. In May Friedman & Shana Calixte (Eds.), *Mothering and blogging: The radical act of the mommyblog* (pp. 57–66). Toronto: Demeter Press.

Gilmore, Leigh. (1994a). *Autobiographics: A feminist theory of women's self-representation*. Ithaca: Cornell University Press.

– (1994b). The mark of autobiography: Postmodernism, autobiography, and genre. In Kathleen Ashley, Leigh Gilmore, & Gerald Peters (Eds.), *Autobiography and postmodernism* (pp. 3–20). Boston: University of Massachusetts Press.

Granju, Katie Allison. (1999). *Attachment parenting: Instinctive care for your baby and young child*. New York: Pocket Books.

Green, Fiona Joy. (2004). Feminist mothers: Successfully negotiating the tension between motherhood as 'institution' and 'experience.' In Andrea O'Reilly (Ed.), *From motherhood to mothering: The legacy of Adrienne Rich's Of Woman Born* (pp. 125–36). Albany: SUNY Press.

– (2009). *Feminist mothering in theory and practice: 1985–1995: A study in transformative politics*. New York: Edwin Mellon Press.

Grossman, Lev, & Hamilton, Anita. (2004, June 13). Meet Joe Blog. *Time Magazine*. Retrieved from http://denisdutton.com/time.htm

Gudmundsdóttir, Gunnthórunn. (2003). *Borderlines: Autobiography and fiction in postmodern life writing*. Amsterdam: Rodopi Press.

Gurak, Laura, Antonijevic, Smiljana, Johnson, Laurie, Ratliff, Clancy, & Reyman, Jessica. (2004). Introduction: Weblogs, rhetoric, community and culture. In Laura Gurak, Smiljana Antonijevic, Laurie Johnson, Clancy Ratliff, & Jessica Reyman (Eds.), *Into the blogosphere: Rhetoric, community and culture of weblogs*. Retrieved from http://blog.lib.umn.edu/blogosphere/.

Halberstam, Judith. (1991). Automating gender: Postmodern feminism in the age of the intelligent machine. *Feminist Studies, 17*(3), 439–60. doi:10.2307/3178281

– (2005). *In a queer place and time: Transgender bodies, subcultural lives*. New York: New York University Press.

Halperin, David N. (1997). *Saint Foucault: Towards a gay hagiography*. New York: Oxford University Press.

– (2003). The normalization of queer theory. *Journal of Homosexuality, 45*(2–4), 339–43. doi:10.1300/J082v45n02_17

Hammond, Lisa. (2010). 'Mommyblogging *is* a radical act': Weblog communities and the construction of maternal identities. In Jocelyn Fenton Stitt & Pegeen Reichart Powell (Eds.), *Mothers who deliver: Feminist interventions into public and interpersonal discourse* (pp. 77–98). Albany: SUNY Press.

Haraway, Donna. (1985, reissued 1991). *Simians, cyborgs and women: The reinvention of nature*. New York: Routledge.

– (1988). Situated knowledges: The science question in feminism and the privilege of partial perspective. *Feminist Studies, 14*(3), 575–99. doi:10.2307/3178066

Harden, B. Garrick. (2009). In blog we trust: An antiphon. In B. Garrick Harden & Robert Carley (Eds.), *Co-opting culture: Culture and power in sociology and cultural studies* (pp. 251–72). Plymouth, UK: Lexington Books.

Hayles, N. Katherine. (2006). Unfinished work: From cyborg to cognisphere. *Theory, Culture & Society, 23*(7–8), 159–66. doi:10.1177/0263276406069229

Hays, Sharon. (1998). *The cultural contradictions of motherhood*. New Haven: Yale University Press.

Herring, Susan C. (2010). Web content analysis: Expanding the paradigm. In Jeremy Hunsinger, Lisbeth Klastrup, & Matthew Allen (Eds.), *International handbook of Internet research* (pp. 233–50). Dordrecht: Springer.

Hill Collins, Patricia. (1987). The meaning of motherhood in Black culture and Black mother-daughter relationships. *Sage: A Scholarly Journal on Black Women 4*(2), 4–11.

Hirsch, Marianne. (1997). *Family frames: Photography, narrative, and postmemory*. Cambridge: Harvard University Press.

Hochman, David. (2005, January 30). Mommy (and me). *The New York Times*. Retrieved from http://www.nytimes.com/2005/01/30/fashion/30moms.html

Jackaman, Rob. (2003). *Broken English/breaking English: A study of contemporary poetries in English*. London: Rosemont.

Kadar, Marlene (Ed.). (1992). *Essays on life writing: From genre to critical practice*. Toronto: University of Toronto Press.

– (Ed.). (1993). *Reading life writing: An anthology*. Toronto: Oxford University Press.

Kadar, Marlene, Warley, Linda, Perreault, Jeanne, & Egan, Susanna (Eds.). (2005). *Tracing the autobiographical*. Waterloo: Wilfred Laurier University Press.

Kaplan, Caren, Alarcón, Norma, & Moallem, Minoo (Eds.). (1999). *Between woman and nation: Nationalisms, transnational feminism and the state*. Durham: Duke University Press.

Karlsson, Lena. (2007). Desperately seeking sameness: The processes and pleasures of identification in women's diary blog reading. *Feminist Media Studies, 7*(2), 137–53. doi:10.1080/14680770701287019

– (2006). Acts of reading diary weblogs. *HumanIT, 8*(2), 1–59.

Kinser, Amber. (2008). Mothering as relational consciousness. In Andrea O'Reilly (Ed.), *Feminist mothering* (pp. 123–42). Albany: SUNY Press.

Knight, India. (2009, November 1) Women's blogging: The new home front. *Times Online*. Retrieved from http://www.ytlcommunity.com/commnews/shownews.asp?newsid=49530

Lather, Patti. (1991). *Getting smart: Feminist research and pedagogy with/in the postmodern*. New York: Routledge.

Lazar, Michelle M. (Ed.). (2005). *Feminist critical discourse analysis: Gender, power and ideology in discourse*. New York: Palgrave

Lejeune, Philippe. (1982). The autobiographical contract. In Tzevetan Todorov (Ed.), *French literary theory today: A reader* (pp. 192–222). New York: Cambridge University Press.

Lemke, Jay. (2008). Identity, development and desire: Critical questions. In Carmen Rosa Caldas-Coulthard & Rick Iedema (Eds.), *Identity trouble: Critical discourse and contested identities* (pp. 17–42). New York: Palgrave, Macmillan.

López, Lori Kido. (2009). The 'radical act' of mommyblogging: Redefining motherhood through the blogosphere. *New Media & Society, 11*(5), 729–47. doi:10.1177/1461444809105349

Lye, John. (1998). Some issues in postcolonial theory: the literature(s) of the colonized. Retrieved from http://www.brocku.ca/english/courses/4F70/postcol.php

Maushart, Susan. (2000). *The mask of motherhood: How becoming a mother changes our lives and why we never talk about it*. New York: Penguin.

McNeill, Laurie. (2003). Teaching an old genre new tricks: The diary on the Internet. *Biography, 26*(1), 24–47. doi:10.1353/bio.2003.0028

Mehra, Bharat, Merkel, Cecelia, & Bishop, Ann Peterson. (2004). The Internet for empowerment of minority and marginalized users. *New Media & Society, 6*(6), 781–802. doi:10.1177/146144804047513

Miller, Carolyn R., & Shepherd, Dawn. (2009). Questions for genre theory from the blogosphere. In Janet Giltrow & Dieter Stein (Eds.), *Theories of genre and their application to Internet communication* (pp. 263–90). Amsterdam: John Benjamins.

Morrison, Aimee. (2010). Autobiography in real time: A genre analysis of personal mommy blogging. *Cyberpsychology: Journal of Psychosocial Research on Cyberspace, 4*(2), article 1. Retrieved from http://www.cyberpsychology.eu/view.php?cisloclanku=2010120801

Morland, Iain, & Willox, Annabelle (Eds.). (2005). *Queer theory.* New York: Palgrave Macmillan.

Naples, Nancy. (2003). *Feminism and method: Ethnography, discourse analysis and activist research.* New York: Routledge.

Nathanson, Jessica, & Tuley, Laura Camile. (2008). *Mother knows best: Talking back to the "experts."* Toronto: Demeter Press.

Nip, Joyce Y. M. (2004). The Queer Sisters and its electronic bulletin board: A study of the internet for social movement mobilization. In Wim Van De Donk, Brian D. Loader, Paul G. Nixon, & Dieter Rucht (Eds.), *Cyberprotest: New media, citizens and social movements* (pp. 233–58). New York: Routledge.

O'Reilly, Andrea (Ed.). (2004). *Mother outlaws: Theories and practices of empowered mothering.* Toronto: Women's Press.

– (Ed.). (2008a). *Feminist mothering.* Albany: SUNY Press.

– (2008b). "This is what feminism is—the acting and living and not just the told": Modeling and mentoring feminism. In Andrea O'Reilly (Ed.), *Feminist mothering* (pp. 191–204). Albany: SUNY Press.

– (2009). The motherhood memoir and the 'New Momism': Biting the hand that feeds you. In Andrea O'Reilly & Silvia Caporale Bizzini (Eds.), *From the personal to the political: Toward a new theory of maternal narrative,* (pp. 238–48). Selinsgrove: Susquehanna University Press.

O'Reilly, Andrea, & Caporale Bizzini, Silvia (Eds.). (2009). *From the personal to the political: Toward a new theory of maternal narrative.* Selinsgrove: Susquehanna University Press.

Park, Shelley. (2010). Cyborg mothering. In Jocelyn Fenton Stitt & Pegeen Reichart Powell (Eds.), *Mothers who deliver: Feminist interventions into public and interpersonal discourse* (pp. 57–76). Albany: SUNY Press.

Payne, Martin. (2006). *Narrative therapy: An introduction for counselors* (2nd ed.). London: Sage Publications.

Podnieks, Elizabeth. (2002). Web diaries, cyber selves and global intimacy: Surfing SecraTerri's *Footnotes*. *a/b: Auto/Biography Studies* 17(1), 119–38.

– (2004). 'I lit sluts' and 'page pimps': Online diarists and their quest for cyber union. *Life Writing*, 1(2), 123–50. doi:10.1080/10408340308518263

Podnieks, Elizabeth, & O'Reilly, Andrea (Eds.). (2010) *Textual mothers/maternal texts: Motherhood in contemporary women's literatures.* Waterloo: Wilfred Laurier University Press.

Probyn, Elspeth. (1996). *Outside belongings.* New York: Routledge.

Rich, Adrienne. (1976, reissued 1995). *Of woman born: Motherhood as experience and institution.* New York: Norton and Company.

Rosenberg, Scott. (2009). *Say everything: How blogging began, what it's becoming and why it matters.* New York: Random House.

Rosenwald, Lawrence A. (1988). *Emerson and the art of the diary.* New York: Oxford University Press.

Ruddick, Sara. (1980, reissued 2007). *Maternal thinking.* In Andrea O'Reilly (Ed.), *Maternal theory: Essential readings* (pp. 96–113). Toronto: Demeter Press.

– (1989, reissued 1995). *Maternal thinking: Toward a politics of peace.* Boston: Beacon Press.

Scott, Joan W. (1992). Experience. In Judith Butler & Joan W. Scott (Eds.), *Feminists theorize the political* (pp. 22–40). New York: Routledge.

Serfaty, Viviane. (2004). *The mirror and the veil: An overview of American online diaries and blogs.* Amsterdam: Rodopi Press.

Servon, Lisa. (2002). *Bridging the digital divide: Technology, community, and public policy.* Malden, MA: Blackwell. doi:10.1002/9780470773529

Shohat, Ella (Ed.). (1998). *Talking visions: Multicultural feminism in a transnational age.* New York: MIT Press.

Shohat, Ella, & Stam, Robert. (1994). *Unthinking Eurocentrism: Multiculturalism and the media.* New York: Routledge.

Sinor, Jennifer. (2002). *The extraordinary work of ordinary writing: Annie Ray's diary.* Iowa City: University of Iowa Press.

Smith, Sidonie, & Watson, Julia (Eds.). (1998). *Women, autobiography, theory: A reader.* Madison, WI: Wisconsin University Press.

– (Eds.). (2001). *Reading autobiography: A guide for interpreting life narratives.* Minneapolis: University of Minnesota Press.

Smith-Windsor, Jaimie. (2004). The cyborg mother: A breached boundary. *Ctheory.* Retrieved from http://www.ctheory.net/articles.aspx?id=409

Sommer, Doris. (1988). Not just a personal story: Women's *testimonios* and the plural self. In Bella Brodzki & Celeste Schenck (Eds.), *Life/lines: Theorizing women's autobiography* (pp. 107–30). Ithaca: Cornell University Press.

Stanford Friedman, Susan. (1988, reissued 1998). Women's autobiographical selves: Theory and practice. In Sidonie Sidonie & Julia Watson (Eds.), *Women, autobiography, theory: A reader* (pp. 72–82). Madison, WI: Wisconsin University Press.

Thurer, Shari. (1994). *The myths of motherhood: How culture reinvents the good mother*. Boston: Houghton Mifflin.

Turner, William B. (2000). *A geneology of queer theory*. Philadelphia: Temple University Press.

van Dijk, Teun A. (2001). Multidisciplinary CDA: A plea for diversity. In Ruth Wodak & Michael Meyer (Eds.), *Methods of critical discourse analysis* (pp. 95–120). London: Sage. doi:10.4135/9780857028020.d7

van Leeuwan, Theo. (2008). Three modes of interdisciplinarity. In Ruth Wodak & Paul Chilton (Eds.), *A new agenda in (critical) discourse analysis: theory, methodology and interdisciplinarity* (pp. 3–18). Amsterdam: John Benjamins Publishing Company.

VNS Matrix. (1991). *Cyberfeminist manifesto*. Retrieved from http://www.sysx .org/gashgirl/VNS/TEXT/PINKMANI.HTM

Volkart, Yvonne. (2004). The cyberfeminist fantasy of the pleasure of the cyborg. In Claudia Reiche & Verena Kuni (Eds.), *Cyberfeminism: Next protocols* (pp. 97–118). Brooklyn: Autonomedia.

Waldman, Ayelet. (2009). *Bad mother: A chronicle of maternal crimes, minor calamities and occasional moments of grace*. New York: Doubleday.

Walker, Alice. (1974, reissued 2007). In search of our mothers' gardens. In Andrea O'Reilly (Ed.), *Maternal theory: Essential readings* (pp. 88–95). Toronto: Demeter Press.

Walker Rettberg, Jill. (2008). *Blogging*. Cambridge, Polity Press.

Warley, Linda. (2005). In Marlene Kadar, Linda Warley, Jeanne Perreault, & Susanna Egan (Eds.), *Tracing the autobiographical* (pp. 25–42). Waterloo: Wilfred Laurier University Press.

Wilson, Matthew W. (2009). Cyborg geographies: Towards hybrid epistemologies. *Gender, Place and Culture, 16*(5), 499–516. doi:10.1080/09663690903148390

Winokur, Mark. (2003). The ambiguous panopticon: Foucault and the codes of cyberspace. *Ctheory*. Retrieved from http://www.ctheory.net/articles .aspx?id=371

Wodak, Ruth, & Meyer, Michael. (2001). *Methods of critical discourse analysis*. London: Sage.

Wolf, Naomi. (2001). *Misconceptions: Truth, lies, and the unexpected on the journey to motherhood.*

Young, Iris Marion. (1990). The ideal of community and the politics of difference. In Linda J. Nicholson (Ed.), *Feminism/postmodernism* (pp. 300–23). New York: Routledge.

Index